"Terry Wilhelm provides a unique perspective on a critical aspect of the PLC process—shared leadership. As the PLC movement continues to proliferate, such guidance is both needed and timely."

Robert J. Marzano, CEO
Marzano Research

"Shared Leadership does an excellent job of providing principals with a step-by-step process for leading change in their schools. Professional Learning Communities are not something schools just have. They have to be developed and nurtured. Terry Wilhelm provides that process with many supportive resources and practices. There is also an excellent research base for the content presented in the book. The best part about this book is that principals have the ability to determine what steps they need to employ, depending on the readiness and development of the staff. There are lots of good suggestions and ideas for leading the entire process, but principals have the ability to take the suggested activities and adapt them to their current situation. This would be a good textbook for school administrator credential programs in preparing school leaders for taking on the change process at their schools."

Glenn Sewell, Assistant Professor of Educational Administration
Sanford College of Education, National University

"The concept of shared leadership is essential to increase student learning, yet the most elusive for school leaders to fully grasp and practice. In Shared Leadership, Terry Wilhelm provides a proven road map for school leaders. This is a must read for anyone who seeks a high quality PLC."

Maureen E. Latham, Superintendent
Beaumont Unified School District

"In my years as a principal and leadership consultant I have always been on the lookout for practical and useful resources that can help school leaders in real time. Terry Wilhelm has provided such a resource. This book is filled with practical guidance and useful tools that can have an immediate impact on a school's culture and ability to meet students' needs. I highly recommend this book!"

Greg Cameron, Learning Crest Partner and Author

"The book's major strength is the credibility of the elegant research from the author's own experiences and well as an extensive discussion of research from the literature. This book would be an excellent resource for the Superintendent of any K–12 school district to use as professional development for district administrators. Of course, the book is a "must" for school principals who are striving to develop school leadership skills among the significant adults in their schools."

Adeline Civretta, Retired Facilitator
California School Leadership Academy, Riverside County, CA

"This is the most comprehensive collection of current research and effective practices for successful, sustainable, school change available. It includes solid, practical guidance on the essential tools and processes needed to take our team's efforts to the next level, and will undoubtedly become our manual for continuous improvement, districtwide."

Anne M. Lundquist, Superintendent
Red Lake School District #38, Minnesota

"I realized many years ago that school leaders cannot accomplish "everything" they need to without help. That help comes in many forms and various avenues. Sharing leadership through professional learning communities empowers leaders from within the organization to step forward and assume both formal and

informal leadership positions with the organization. In this book, you will see how shared leadership can improve your school."

Dr. B.J. Worthington, Director of Schools
Clarksville-Montgomery County School System

"Terry Wilhelm's insight—rooted in extensive practice, inquiry, and research—brings 21st century educational leadership into realistic focus, while demonstrating the unique and essential qualities of collaboration. The author provides a vision of and practical tools to assist in the implementation of a principle-based, shared leadership model that creates conditions resulting in high student achievement."

Gregory Kampf, Superintendent, (Retired)
Lompoc Unified SD

"Every principal and every administrator who supervises principals with the goal of improving student outcomes through shared leadership and PLCs in their schools should read this book. It is packed with practical how-tos based on the author's real-time experience working with school teams for over 15 years. There's so much here...Terry has thought of just about everything to help principals and teachers grow professionally and to transform their schools for the benefit of their students."

Dr. Kathy Wright, Superintendent (Retired)
Alvord USD

"We've long known that culture is the "secret sauce" of school improvement—with it, anything is possible; without it, nothing is possible. Yet getting from a dysfunctional school culture to a high-performing one is no small feat. Terry Wilhelm's book is full of practical tools and guidance for doing exactly that and reflects solid research from McREL and others about effective school leadership. This book is a must for leadership teams grappling with what is often the most difficult aspect of school improvement—creating a purposeful community that's committed to continuous improvement."

Bryan Goodwin, President & CEO
McREL International

Shared Leadership

For Holly and Toby.

Shared Leadership

*The Essential Ingredient
for Effective PLCs*

Terry Wilhelm

CORWIN
A SAGE Publishing Company

FOR INFORMATION:

Corwin

A SAGE Company

2455 Teller Road

Thousand Oaks, California 91320

(800) 233-9936

www.corwin.com

SAGE Publications Ltd.

1 Oliver's Yard

55 City Road

London EC1Y 1SP

United Kingdom

SAGE Publications India Pvt. Ltd.

B 1/I 1 Mohan Cooperative Industrial Area

Mathura Road, New Delhi 110 044

India

SAGE Publications Asia-Pacific Pte. Ltd.

3 Church Street

#10-04 Samsung Hub

Singapore 049483

Executive Acquisitions Editor: Arnis Burvikovs

Senior Associate Editor: Desiree A. Bartlett

Senior Editorial Assistant: Andrew Olson

Production Editor: Libby Larson

Copy Editor: Deanna Noga

Typesetter: C&M Digitals (P) Ltd.

Proofreader: Theresa Kay

Indexer: Will Ragsdale

Cover Designer: Karine Hovsepian

Marketing Manager: Anna Marie Mesick

Copyright © 2017 by Corwin

Printed in the United States of America.

Library of Congress Cataloging-in-Publication Data

Names: Wilhelm, Terry, author.

Title: Shared leadership : the essential ingredient for effective PLCs / Terry Wilhelm.

Description: Thousand Oaks, California : Corwin, A SAGE Company, 2017. | Includes bibliographical references and index.

Identifiers: LCCN 2016008145 | ISBN 9781506311227 (pbk. : alk. paper)

Subjects: LCSH: Professional learning communities—United States. | Teacher-principal relationships—United States. | Teacher participation in administration—United States.

Classification: LCC LB1731 .W428 2017 | DDC 370.71/1—dc23 LC record available at https://lccn.loc.gov/2016008145

This book is printed on acid-free paper.

Certified Chain of Custody
Promoting Sustainable Forestry
www.sfiprogram.org
SFI-01268

SFI label applies to text stock

16 17 18 19 20 10 9 8 7 6 5 4 3 2 1

Contents

Access links and additional resources at
www.corwin.com/sharedleadership

LIST OF RESOURCES ON THE COMPANION WEBSITE

 Access links and additional resources at
www.corwin.com/sharedleadership

Forms and Tools

Chapter 1
Confidential Principal Tool for Selection of Guiding Coalition

Chapter 2
Principal Self-Assessment for Shared Leadership Readiness

Chapter 4
Agenda
Role Tent Cards
Parking Lot
The Talking Stick
What Is a Professional Learning Community (PLC)?
Questions of a PLC
School-Wide Roles
Our Team Compact (Sample)
Five Steps to Effective Norms
Professional Work Plan and Team Commitments
Tool Kit

Chapter 6
Agenda
After Action Review
Collaboration Survey for Course-Alike Teams
Collaboration Survey for Vertical Teams or Teams of Specialists

Chapter 7
Agenda
Writing or Evaluating a Mission Statement
Headlines-Our Vision
Collective Commitments

p. 89 (pdf) *The Balanced Leadership Framework: Connecting Vision With Action* (2007) by Tim Waters and Greg Cameron

http://files.eric.ed.gov/fulltext/ED544245.pdf

p. 109 (Video) *Tuning Protocol: Fine Tuning Our Classroom Practice With Presenting Teacher Donn Cushing*

https://www.youtube.com/watch?v=OnI5MMLC5MA

p. 109 (Video) *Tuning Protocol: Fine Tuning Our Classroom Practice With Presenting Teacher Gareth Richards*

https://www.youtube.com/watch?v=u_HodYR1k-Q&list=LLM5M_WXsfc9mqD6aqbSqmDg&index=1

p. 119 (Video) *Student-Based Protocol*

https://www.youtube.com/watch?v=VKZb77-Yz44

p. 119 (Video) *Elementary Math Data Protocol*

https://www.youtube.com/watch?v=9e6CNbaEvKw

p. 146 (Article) *Stealthy Interventions* (2015) by Terry Wilhelm

http://education.cu-portland.edu/blog/leaders-link/just-for-aps-stealthy-interventions/

p. 162 (Article) *We're Already a "Good" School - Why Do We Have to Improve?* (2007) by Richard DuFour

http://www.allthingsplc.info/blog/view/16/wersquore-already-a-good-school-why-do-we-need-to-improve

p. 164 (Article) Teachers vs. Administrators: Ending the Adversarial Relationship (2013) by Terry Wilhelm

http://education.cu-portland.edu/blog/leaders-link/teachers-vs-administrators-ending-the-adversarial-relationship/

For Further Reading
Sharing Leadership in PD Best Practices (2015) by Terry Wilhelm

http://education.cu-portland.edu/blog/leaders-link/shared-leadership-best-practices/

Making a Difference, One Child at a Time (2009) by Terry Wilhelm

http://www.educators2000.com/pdf-articles/Leadership%20-%20One%20at%20a%20time%20Article.pdf

Professional Reading Protocols in a
PD Setting - Six-part series
• Part I: Full vs. Abbreviated Jigsaw
http://education.cu-portland.edu/blog/leaders-links/principal-as-staff-developer-the-jigsaw-and-its-alternatives/

• Part II: Reading Cascade
http://education.cu-portland.edu/blog/leaders-link/principal-as-staff-developer-the-jigsaw-and-its-alternatives-part-two/

- Part III: "Final Word" Discussion Protocol
http://education.cu-portland.edu/blog/leaders-link/principal-as-staff-developer-alternatives-to-the-jigsaw-part-3/

- Part IV: "Chunked and Timed" Protocol
http://education.cu-portland.edu/blog/leaders-link/principal-as-staff-developer-alternatives-to-the-jigsaw-part-four/

- Part V: Partner Reading
http://education.cu-portland.edu/blog/leaders-link/principal-as-staff-developer-alternatives-to-the-jigsaw-part-five/

- Part VI: Use of Margin Notes and Varying Levels of Sharing Out
http://education.cu-portland.edu/blog/leaders s-link/principal-as-staff-developer-alternatives-to-the-jigsaw-part-six/

Facilitation Notes

(Chapter 4)	Getting Started
(Chapter 6)	More Best Practice Meeting Routines, Essential Learnings and Common Assessments
(Chapter 7)	Mission, Vision, Collective Commitments
(Chapter 10)	Student Work Protocol
(Chapter 11)	Student-Based Protocol
(Chapter 12)	Planning-Problem Solving Protocol
(Chapter 13)	Goal Setting and SMARTe Goals
(Chapter 15)	Student Interventions
(Chapter 16)	Working With Challenging Individuals
(Chapter 17)	Leading as Optimizers and Affirmers for Collective Efficacy

Preface

Why This Book?

The market is brimming with books on the topic of professional learning communities (PLCs). However, in my work with school teams, I have found none that address the topic of shared leadership in a PLC. While I was writing this book, a friend who is a retired middle school teacher remarked, "We tried PLCs at our school, and they didn't work." Her comment—incidentally, illustrating a common misconception about what a professional learning community is—echoes many I have heard.

I see many schools begin the PLC journey with great enthusiasm. Why does it sometimes fade so quickly, with the school reverting to its traditional patterns? In my observation, there are two reasons. First, shared decision making has not developed beyond a surface level, mostly involving administrivia, which is a waste of teachers' time and expertise, with no impact on student learning. Second, the principal typically has not provided the teacher leaders with the tools needed to lead teams of colleagues, which requires an investment of regularly scheduled time, just as the collaborative teacher teams must have regularly scheduled time for working together in new ways.

The purpose of this book is to serve as a guide for principals. In 2012, ASCD solicited an article from me, published in *Educational Leadership*, October 2013—an issue devoted to teacher leadership. During the peer review process for "How Principals Cultivate Shared Leadership," the reviewers pressed for a *sequence* of professional learning that principals should provide for teacher leaders. I satisfied their request with a seven-step sequence that appeared in an inset box, but I was not satisfied. The steps made the process appear overly simplistic and somewhat lockstep. This book is the result of developing and elaborating that flexible sequence into a guide. It focuses on developing shared leadership in the areas of curriculum, instruction, and assessment (CIA) through developing teacher leaders' expertise in leading teams of peers and through the functioning of this team of teacher leaders as both an advisory and a decision-making body. Time should only be spent on operational concerns where they impact CIA, in which case teacher leaders' input and/or shared leadership action with the principal is called for.

PRINCIPALS NEED A RESOURCE ■

In 1991, Richard DuFour wrote, "Too often, principals have looked upon staff development as a secondary consideration, an aspect of the operation of the school which warranted little, if any, of their time and attention." The book was *The Principal as Staff Developer*, which connected professional development of teachers—by the principal—to the gold standard in educational leadership strategies of the day: clinical supervision. More than two decades later, clinical supervision remains a respected practice, and formal observation remains a required feature of teacher evaluation, mandated in contracts across the country. But more current research, such as that of Carroll, Fulton, and Doerr (2010), Hattie (2009, 2015), and Hord, Lloyd, Roussin, and Sommers (2010), compels us to work from a new paradigm that is both more effective and more efficient: professional learning communities. But in many schools—in the absence of a district's or area service agency's professional development program—the responsibility for developing teachers as leaders to create a PLC still falls to none other than the principal.

New books are emerging on teacher leadership, as are teacher leadership certification programs—both very positive developments. However, these assume that amid the myriad expectations and responsibilities placed on today's principals, they have also managed to somewhere acquire the know-how for developing teachers as leaders within a cohesive culture of community, then for sharing leadership with them appropriately. At the very least, they assume that principals will *allow* teacher leadership to develop and will allocate meaningful roles to teacher leaders beyond the traditions of department chair, grade level chair, or academic coach/mentor. Realistically, an effective teacher leadership certification program needs a parallel track for the principals, with many intersecting sessions to ensure the development of a cohesive, shared leadership model. *Principals* must lead the work of improving their schools; teacher leadership cannot be developed in a vacuum and have a meaningful school-wide impact. The ideal program is to develop shared leadership together in a team model, with principal and teacher leaders attending the sessions together.

To be certain, many books for developing a school as a professional learning community are available. In 2015, Richard DuFour's book *In Praise of American Educators and How They Can Become Even Better* synthesized the essential elements of all his previous works, refuting the negative media image of U.S. schools while acknowledging the significant challenges they face, with a review of PLC processes as the path to an improved future, but emphasizing the importance of high fidelity to those processes. In the final chapter, DuFour touches on shared leadership, discussing "dispersing leadership," especially among team leaders.

The body of research on shared leadership in education is growing. However, in the absence of a comprehensive shared leadership development program for school teams, I have found no guidebook for principals with the *how-tos* for fostering shared leadership in a school setting, despite the fact that "principal as staff developer" remains an inescapable role for principals who understand the need for their schools to begin operating as PLCs, with teachers assuming a substantially different role in leadership outside their own classrooms. The concept of learning organizations originated in business. For business leaders, this is not a new concept, and a body of literature on shared leadership does exist for them.

HOW TO USE THIS BOOK ■

This book is devoted to outlining and describing, in a flexible sequence, specific practices and processes a principal can use to develop shared leadership in a PLC. It begins with selecting the right team, then proceeds to team agendas designed to develop the teacher leaders' expertise in just-in-time fashion for leading teams of colleagues. The sequence is what I typically use with school teams, but the meetings purposefully are not numbered. You may wish to re-sequence them or add your own agendas. Foundational elements of a PLC are addressed in the outlined guiding coalition (GC) meetings—norms and other teamwork tools; essential learnings and common assessments; mission, vision, commitments, goals; and student interventions. Depending on your school, you may wish to set aside some of the other agendas for now. For example, the chapters on discussion protocols represent a powerful set of tools that accelerate effective collaboration more rapidly than almost any single strategy. But as you work with your teacher leaders in shared leadership, you may decide as a GC that at the present time resistance would outweigh the benefits of introducing them. Or conversely, that most teams are far beyond needing them. Choose what you will use based on your own and your teacher leaders' judgment.

Reproducible tools and agenda notes are provided for each GC meeting. The online resources contain more detailed facilitation notes for principals who would like more structured support with planning and facilitating. Many of these resources can be found as editable Word documents on the book companion website www.corwin.com/sharedleadership Chapters outlining GC meetings conclude with principal follow-up suggestions, and many include troubleshooting tips. Troubleshooting often rests on principals developing and refining their abilities to balance their leadership, whether to be "loose" or "tight" in the nomenclature of the DuFours and their colleagues (2010), or to "step up" versus "step back" in the work of Waters and Cameron (2007). Site administrators face these dilemmas frequently in the development of shared leadership. I believe this is part of the reason that developing shared leadership is, in a sense, more complex, and in its early stages, sometimes even more labor intensive than being the Lone Ranger principal. Yet principals today can no longer lead in ways that accomplish outcomes of significance for all students if they are acting in that outdated role.

ADDITIONAL RESOURCES ■

On the companion website for *Shared Leadership: The Essential Ingredient for Effective PLCs*, you will find many resources. These include downloadable versions of the forms and tools in this book (Forms and Tools), links to related articles referred to in the chapters (Resource Articles and Videos), and highly detailed facilitation notes to augment the Agenda Notes in the chapters containing meeting agendas (Facilitation Notes). The book's References and Resources are also included so that you may access web links.

Acknowledgments

My deepest thanks to Adeline Civretta, Judy Cunningham, Debbie Fay, and Lisa Marin for their enthusiastic support. I greatly appreciate the hours they spent reading my drafts and providing feedback. They are not only professional colleagues, but also personal friends and have been "critical friends" to me in the truest sense throughout this endeavor. Finally, I am enduringly grateful to Rick and Becky DuFour for their encouragement and support since the very inception of this project.

PUBLISHER'S ACKNOWLEDGMENTS ◼

Corwin gratefully acknowledges the contributions of the following reviewers:

Lydia Adegbola
Assistant Principal
New York City Department
of Education
New York, NY

David G. Daniels
Principal
Susquehanna Valley Senior
High School
Conklin, NY

Julie Duford
5th Grade Teacher and PLC
Team Leader
Polson Middle School
Polson, MT

Katina Keener
Principal
Achilles Elementary
School
Hayes, VA

Nancy J. Larsen
Teacher; Adjunct Faculty
University of Idaho; Coeur d'Alene
Charter Academy
Coeur d'Alene, ID

Tanna Nicely
Principal
South Knoxville Elementary
Blaine, TN

Alan Penrose
Assistant Principal; Adjunct
Professor of Education
North Kansas City School District;
Rockhurst University
Kansas City, MO

Ronald W. Poplau
High School Instructor
Shawnee Mission Northwest High
School
Kansas City, KS

About the Author

 Terry Wilhelm, MA, has served as a teacher, principal, district office and area service agency administrator, and university adjunct professor in educational leadership. Her work with principals and school leadership teams spans over 15 years and is the basis for this book. K–12 urban, rural, and suburban schools of all sizes are represented in her work with teams. During her service at the Riverside County Office of Education in Riverside, California, she was Administrator, then Director of the Riverside County School Leadership Center of the California School Leadership Academy (CSLA). When she was appointed Director, Educational Leadership Services, she continued the former CSLA School Leadership Teams (SLT) program, reengineered to support schools working to become professional learning communities. Between 2003 and 2012, 56 schools from 10 districts that participated in SLT met the criteria for inclusion on allthingsplc.info. An external evaluator determined that achievement at these schools exceeded that of similar non-program schools in the county and state, and that they sustained their improvement trajectories after participating in the 2-year program for the duration of the study. Wilhelm has authored many articles on school improvement and is a regular contributor to *Leadership*, the journal of the Association of California School Administrators. Her weekly column, Leaders' Link, written from 2013 to 2016 for HotChalk, Inc. can accessed at http://education.cu-portland.edu/category/blog/leaders-link/. She is a national consultant as well as the founder and owner of Educators2000.com

Introduction

THE NEED ■

We face the urgent and compelling need for a polar shift in school leadership: from the principal as lone leader, to a model of shared leadership between the principal and teacher leaders. The age of the global marketplace, with its demands for graduates who are competitively college and career ready, has overlapped—although not eclipsed—the age of accountability where a schools' worth is measured by test scores. The advent of the Common Core State Standards, or other, newly revised standards in some states, has brought both increased potential to meet the new demands and the heightened challenge of implementing yet another large-scale initiative. The principal can no longer lead this work alone. Researchers led by Timothy Waters at Mid-Continent Research for Education and Learning (2009a) stated, "The future demands on the school principal are massive. In order to meet the needs of all stakeholders, the principal needs to learn to share leadership responsibilities while understanding the implications of introducing change."

Some schools have made, or are making, the shift to shared leadership already. This is evidenced by the fact that, by a variety of measures, including but not limited to test scores, they have become increasingly effective in ensuring that all students, regardless of home background, leave the system fully prepared for college and the global 21st century workforce. They have become constantly improving learning organizations, led by a principal who is a "learning leader." The concept of professional learning communities (PLCs) has become widely used and embraced, thanks to the seminal work of leaders such as Richard and Rebecca DuFour, who have educated thousands in the concept and processes.

The PLC structure has become well documented as a vehicle for improving schools, compellingly evidenced in the meta-analytical research of John Hattie (2009). But Richard DuFour stated to *Phi Delta Kappan* editor Joan Richardson (2011), "Research is not a good driver (of change in school); practice is. My belief is that you should immerse yourself in practice first and then plug yourself into research second." The purpose of this book is to serve as a *practitioner's* guide for principals who are ready to transition to shared leadership.

Accordingly, those who want to know more about the practice can go to www.allthingsplc.info and click on "See the Evidence" for an ever-growing cohort of schools—currently over 200—from the United States and Canada that have been practicing those processes.

PLC processes have come to be recognized as cutting-edge educational reform. When a principal takes a group of teachers to a PLC conference, they are likely to leave with something approaching evangelical fire to transform their school. The road is actually not that complicated. It is not an exotic departure from what we know as schooling. In many respects, it is actually fairly simple. But like many simple things, it can be unexpectedly hard to do. Once the team returns to campus, the sheer daily demands of teaching for the teachers, and running the school for the administrators, may overwhelm their initial enthusiasm and best intentions.

Becoming a PLC requires some structural shifts in the use of resources—time, money, and people. However, more significant are the cultural shifts necessary to enable the structural shifts to occur. The most successful leaders and schools address both structure and culture simultaneously.

■ FROM TRADITIONAL SCHOOLING TO A PLC

In the culture of traditional schooling, the principal, sometimes with an administrative team, runs the show. He or she directs the production, and teachers play their assigned instructional roles in their autonomous, individual classrooms. A foundational structure for schools that are becoming PLCs is the formation of teacher-led teams of teachers who accomplish specific kinds of work interdependently—all in support of the overall school mission, vision, and goals—but typically with no administrator present. This may be a new structure for some schools, where department meetings or traditional grade-level meetings have been the norm since the dawn of living memory.

Unfortunately, teacher preparation programs historically have offered nothing to prepare teachers to lead teams of peers in these new kinds of group tasks: analyzing student work and achievement data, facilitating discussions about improved instructional practices to produce better learning, comparing results for various tried strategies, putting structures in place to hold each other accountable for trying and using the strategies, and the development of classroom and team level student interventions for the short and longer terms.

Expecting teachers to know how to collaborate in this high-level fashion reminds me of myself as a young teacher expecting my students to know how to work in cooperative groups. They didn't! Each table group task quickly deteriorated into arguing, sulking, and one or two students doing all the work. After trying this a few times, I just gave up and put the desks back into rows. It took some honest self-examination to stop blaming them for being so uncooperative and accept the fact that they needed *instruction and practice* in the skills of cooperative learning from me—just as they did for academics! Also, I liked being in charge—after all, I was the teacher, right?

In time, I got better—and so did they! I introduced cooperative skills and they practiced them *while* they worked on math, language arts, and other subjects. Key to our success was my ability to see my own role differently. The parallel I am attempting to draw is that principals may likewise have trouble relinquishing control and may also need to develop a whole new skill set to develop their teachers as leaders.

I have also observed the opposite extreme—misguided principals abdicating important aspects of leadership, leaving to their wholly unprepared leadership teams vital school-wide decisions and responsibilities.

Shared Leadership Is Not Delegation

Shared leadership involves sharing some decision-making and other responsibilities, but it is not abdication, and it is quite different than simple delegation. Assuredly, there are certain routine tasks and responsibilities that a principal can and should delegate to experienced staff members, including classified staff. But developing the depth of *shared* leadership necessary for transforming a school into a PLC so that all students can achieve at the highest levels is very different. It is not an event or an action, like delegating a task to someone. It is a developmental process. It does not happen overnight or in a few months. Deliberately planned, developmentally shared leadership will be more effective after 2 years than after 1 and will continue to blossom and grow—along with student outcomes—the longer it is thoughtfully and intentionally fostered.

Principals who have taken this journey describe it as a rewarding adventure; seeing their teachers develop as leaders is intensely satisfying. Shared leadership is transformative for teachers, but its ultimate beneficiaries are the students. Today's school leaders have a moral imperative to lead differently and more effectively, and shared leadership is the vehicle.

1

The Right Team

Most schools already have a team designated as the Leadership Team. At the secondary level this typically consists of the department chairs, and for elementary, grade-level chairs/leads. Selection of members varies by school—perhaps they are voted in by peers; perhaps responsibility rotates annually from one team member to another.

Knowing this, it makes sense to carefully consider the makeup of the team that will begin to share leadership with you to begin moving the school—or accelerate the progress—toward becoming a professional learning community. This group will become key in all improvement efforts. It is all-important to create a team that is open and ready to make this role shift, with members willing to de-privatize their own practice, while stepping up to lead peers in work that will do likewise. One of my colleagues who had been a high school principal for 20 years was fond of saying, "In schools, all the decisions are made for the comfort and convenience of the adults." The teachers you select should be those who already put student needs ahead of their own and their colleagues' comfort and convenience.

This is not a group of "yes-men" or "yes-women," but choosing difficult personalities or those who perpetually play devil's advocate will derail the shared leadership train before it departs. Someone who is occasionally skeptical, helping the team see all sides of a decision, can be a good addition. A perpetual blocker is not.

In some schools, the current, standing leadership team may not be the right group for this new role. Although some principals might feel that it is politically difficult to select a new team specifically for this purpose, it is important to weigh pros and cons before simply deciding to keep the status quo. In schools I have supported, the most successful teams—whose schools progress farther in less time—are new teams formed specifically for the work of leading their schools on the journey toward becoming a professional learning community (PLC). Typically, new teams include some teachers who are also part of the standing leadership team and others who are new members.

Consider the larger picture: Every teacher in the school is—or will be—part of a collaborative team, with each team led by a teacher leader who is part of the new group you are creating to share leadership with you. For elementary schools, each grade level becomes a collaborative team. For secondary, the teachers who teach each major *course*—U.S. history, biology, seventh-grade English—will be a team. A discussion of assigning teachers who have multiple preps will be covered in Team Assignments and Leader Selection. A comprehensive high school may have between 20 and 25 collaborative teams.

If you select a new team, it is advisable to call it by a new name to distinguish it from the traditional leadership team that will remain in place. The new group might be called the Guiding Coalition, or the Steering Committee.

Some principals have felt it advisable to leave the term *professional learning community* or *PLC* out of the new team's title. New terms become buzzwords, and buzzwords and acronyms notoriously take on various meanings and interpretations to different constituents, and these have suffered that fate as well.

The standing leadership team will continue to function, overall, in its traditional role. In some districts, such as the Beaumont Unified School District in Beaumont, California, new school teams formed for this work were named the Instructional Leadership Council, or ILC. The traditional elementary grade-level chairs (GLCs) continued in many of their former functions, in some cases sharing responsibilities with ILC members at their grade levels. Secondary department chairs in Beaumont also continued to function in a traditional fashion, with some also becoming ILC members.

Members of your new team *must* be highly respected by colleagues. Because they need to have attained credibility with peers, they should not be the newest, least experienced teachers, even though such teachers often have very positive attitudes and openness to new challenges. Those chosen should be strong, effective teachers, but it is especially important for them to possess an attitude of openness to their own continuous improvement and to the role of leading colleagues in new ways.

For purposes of this book, I use the term *guiding coalition* or *GC*. Each GC member will facilitate specific kinds of work with his or her collaborative team.

As mentioned, a teacher could be *both* a GC member and a department chair/grade-level chair. *Over time*, since traditional leadership team members are typically voted in or otherwise selected for one to two years, it may be desirable for the criteria for being on the leadership team to eventually be modified (if possible) to include being a GC member, thus streamlining the functioning of the two groups and eliminating the need for separate meetings.

Since many secondary teachers have multiple preps, I recommend prioritizing team participation—*before* determining GC leadership—according to the highest-leverage courses these teachers teach (see Team Assignments and Leader Selection). As collaboration becomes more sophisticated, strategies can be developed to publish the work of each course-alike team with all teachers who may teach one or more sections of that course, but who are assigned to other teams.

For singletons, such as a band teacher, a full-time ceramics teacher, and other such specialized teachers, an interdisciplinary "specialists' team" or "enhancement subjects team" can be formed. It is absolutely essential that every teacher on staff is part of a team. One mistake secondary principals sometimes make is to excuse these teachers—or other noncore teachers, such as PE teachers—from team membership. The result is a badly mixed message, symbolically undercutting the importance of team collaboration and undermining their own statements of the value of forming a cohesive, school-wide learning community. Other configurations for specialists are possible, including teams that collaborate electronically or whose members—from various schools—meet in a central location. These configurations have issues of their own, however, and having all teams from a school collaborating with others *at* their own school lends strength to the model of the school as a PLC. More on teams of single-subject specialists in Chapters 5, 9, and 10.

As mentioned, a comprehensive high school could have between 20 and 25 collaborative teams, each with its own teacher leader, while in very small elementary schools, where there may be only one or one-and-a-half classes (combinations) at each grade level, teams may be vertical combinations, such as K–1, 2–3, and 4–6.

Some specialists—such as special education teachers—are often best assigned to a specific grade level in elementary schools, and a specific course-alike team at the secondary level. They bring extensive expertise to the teams they join, and if they belong to a team where many of their students are enrolled (as Resource Specialist Program [RSP] students) or mainstreamed (from a Special Day Class [SDC]), they are an important voice in the team's planning. Even if few or no students from an SDC are currently mainstreamed, it is valuable for the SDC teacher to interact with other teachers who share the content he or she is providing—with appropriate accommodations and modifications—for his or her own students.

Course-alike, vertical, and interdisciplinary teams all have specific advantages when used for various purposes. Based on the size of the school, having as many teachers as possible on course-alike teams forms a solid foundation for teamwork. Then, other configurations can be used strategically, for specific purposes, once teaming is established.

The chapter on goal setting with SMARTe goals will further explore what it takes to make a group of teachers a *team*.

To guide your thinking process for team selection, see the Confidential Principal Tool for Selection of Guiding Coalition.

TEAM ASSIGNMENTS AND LEADER SELECTION ■

Recommended Prioritizing Strategy for Collaborative Team Participation (prior to GC selection) at the Secondary Level

Step 1—Assign English and mathematics teachers to one team each

    1a—Eliminate any other subjects from these teachers' potential team lists, even if they have more preps of the other courses

1b—High school—ninth grade has top priority; other grade levels in descending order (e.g., a teacher teaching ninth and tenth will be assigned to the ninth-grade team) (Algebra takes precedence over Geometry, and so on)

1b—Middle school—assign by greatest number of preps, but ensuring that each team has sufficient membership to make a team

Step 2—Assign science and social studies teachers to one team each

2a—Eliminate any other subjects from these teachers' potential team lists, even if they have more preps of the other courses

2b—High school—ninth-grade courses have top priority; other grade levels in descending order—see Step 1

2b—Middle school—assign by greatest number of preps, but ensure that each team has sufficient membership to make a team

Step 3—Assign all teachers who teach NO sections of core subjects

3a—Use grade levels first, if the overall subject group is large (e.g., ninth-grade PE)

3b—Consider groupings such as performing arts, fine arts, or career tech if there are sufficient members to create more job-alike teams

For very small secondary schools, create English and mathematics teams first, then science and social studies, then all others. This is a similar structure to vertical teams at very small elementary schools.

Obviously this prioritizing strategy will vary by school, numbers of teachers in potential teams, and individual principal judgment—including judgments about individual teachers' personalities and interactions with specific peers, although this should *not* be the first pass deciding factor.

English and mathematics courses are key to student success in all other subjects, and thus receive first priority for any teacher who teaches even one section. For high school, further rationale for this method lies in the fact that ninth graders are most at risk of school failure, with older students less at risk, overall, as they age. So in assigning teachers to collaborative teams that will interactively plan for student success, it is important to prioritize team assignments that serve younger students first.

Note: The Essential Program Components (EPCs) of the Academic Program Survey (APS) in California (Department of Education, 2013) are a research-based set of recommendations that are applied to schools not meeting Adequate Yearly Progress for Title I. Applying the priorities discussed above to the allocation of resources—in this case, teacher expertise—have enabled schools that apply them faithfully to make significant improvement in student outcomes.

Confidential Principal Tool
for Selection of Guiding Coalition

Important Note: Complete all staff team assignments first—see previous section.

There is no answer key or recommended total score for these ratings. This tool is to help create a profile of each teacher under consideration as a GC member. Ideally, you want team members with 4s and 5s. Remember that this team will have to work *together* as a team, in addition to each leading their own teams, so consider the group dynamics of the GC you are building. See sample teacher P. Smith.

(This form should be duplicated for secondary use, because multiple candidates may need to be considered to select the optimum leader for each team. Elementary principals will consider candidates for selecting one GC leader for each team, preK or kindergarten through sixth grade.)

Confidential Principal Tool for Selection of Guiding Coalition

Confidential principal perception ratings: 1 = Low; 5 = High

Name of potential GC team leader	Current member of Leadership Team (department or grade-level chair)? (Yes/no)	Number of years teaching and number of years at site (Yrs/Yrs)	Overall openness to new school and classroom practices (Rating)	Overall positive attitude (Rating)	Overall ability to analyze, discuss, and present new ideas about school and classroom practices (Rating)	Overall strength as a classroom teacher (most students succeeding) (Rating)	Overall openness to feedback about personal teaching practices (Rating)	Overall credibility with peers on assigned team (Rating)
P. Smith for [team]	No	7/3	5	4	5	4	5	5

SUMMARY ■

Choosing the right team is foundational to the success of beginning shared leadership. In most cases, the standing leadership team is not the right team for this purpose. After considering adjustments that may be needed in the makeup of teams school-wide—specifically for secondary—use the suggested tool to select the optimum candidates for team leadership. These teacher leaders will become your guiding coalition.

Access links and additional resources at
www.corwin.com/sharedleadership

2

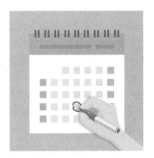

Creating the Calendar and Reflecting on Readiness

Taking the time to prepare thoroughly for the first meeting of your guiding coalition will pay off with each subsequent meeting.

CREATING THE CALENDAR ■

When is the best time of year to begin this work? The best time is now. Waiting until September has no advantages, other than the fact that it *feels* like a new beginning. There can actually be good reasons not to start in September, including a plethora of other new district or site initiatives, typically rolled out with a new school year. In my many years of working with school teams, I have seen that one of the most practical, helpful aspects of becoming a professional learning community (PLC) is that it brings all the curricular, instructional, and assessment initiatives into a coherent model, including new ones as they come down the pike. Thus, any time can be optimal for beginning the work.

As more schools nationwide join the PLC journey, it has become increasingly common for teacher contracts to prescribe regularly scheduled time for collaboration during the work day. This is absolutely essential. Without time for regular collaboration carved out of the contract day, a PLC is, at best, a part-time, half-hearted endeavor that will produce similar results—along with a lot of teacher frustration, especially on the part of teacher leaders. Uninterrupted, diligently protected time for collaboration of at least 45 to 60 minutes per week is a good start. Some secondary schools now have master schedules with daily common prep periods for teachers by teams. Thus, these teachers have the potential for collaborating several times weekly. A fascinating phenomenon of teacher collaboration is that although some may resist in the beginning, the more they collaborate (and improve their collaborative skills) the more they like it. In the long run, collaboration reduces teacher isolation, spreads the workload, and saves individual teacher preparation time. Most important, everyone's students become more successful—the very purpose of collaborating.

Ironically, the juncture of excitement over winning time for collaboration during the school day is the very point at which the journey often falters. Negotiating collaboration time as a contractual feature is sometimes a long, even arduous process. But once this is accomplished, there is a sadly mistaken assumption that nothing more needs to be done. *The missed point is that it is equally critical for the teacher leaders—your guiding coalition (GC)—to have regular, protected time to work and learn together as a team.* It is impossible to overstate this. This is a widely ignored necessity and slows the development of many schools on their journeys. This is where leadership skills are proactively taught, practiced, and discussed in an emotionally safe setting. This is where you, the principal, begin to symbolically and concretely share decision making. This is where you learn what is working and what is floundering—across the whole school—in one setting. This is where, with the help of the teacher leaders, you develop and coalesce your own thinking—and statements you will make to the staff as a whole—about what you will be tight on and what you will be loose on. It is time that is absolutely critical to the development of this team and its members, including yourself as the leader of the leaders. Think of the oxygen mask speech during takeoff on a commercial airline: put your own mask on first, then help others who may need assistance. This regular, protected time is when the GC recharges itself so that its members can go forth and provide leadership to their colleagues.

How much time do you need for this purpose, and how often? Weekly is ideal; monthly is probably the minimum for progress to be made. An hour to 90 minutes weekly will accomplish a great deal; a half-day monthly would probably work. The same kinds of strategies used to carve out time for teacher collaboration can also be applied to find time for the GC to work together. Remember that GC time *does not replace* team collaboration—it is, essentially, preparation for it. In my experience, among the easiest ways of finding GC time is to pay teachers for the additional hourly time before or after school, or to build a common prep period into the master schedule where all GC members are available at the same time during the school day.

I worked with one high school principal who lamented, "I have no time for this [GC] team to get together, and it's killing us!"

I asked, "Could you pay them?" She stopped in her tracks and shook her head as if to shake out the cobwebs.

"That was too simple. That's a 'duh.'" And that is what she did.

So the first step is to create the calendar. The calendar needs to include the regular teacher collaboration dates and times each month (ideally, once a week) AND the GC meetings that will support that work. Once your GC is identified, they will help you refine the calendar—a symbolic beginning of shared leadership.

What is the agenda for these GC meetings? That is the content of this book. Each chapter focuses on one GC meeting's content, designed to support the teacher leaders as they lead their upcoming team meetings. The GC meeting for that content could be one session, or multiple sessions that span a number of collaborative meetings that your teacher leaders will lead. Both the time frames and sequence suggested in this book are flexible and should be adapted to your own context, but they are based on the work of real teams, at all levels, observed and analyzed for over 15 years.

I hasten to add that there is no ideal or perfect sequence of developmental activities for these GC sessions. In my work, I create customized sessions for each cohort of teams, based on their levels of understanding and real application of the processes. Countless school principals in areas where the PLC concept has become popular have proudly informed me, "We've been doin' PLCs for ___ years!" A short conversation may reveal that their school has been doing what has been termed "PLC Lite"—teachers meet at least occasionally in what are referred to as "teams," but what goes on during those meetings has little coherence. Also, the school's Pyramid Response to Intervention may be so ill-defined that many students are falling through the cracks. Conversations with teachers are the most telling—do they see their work as being all about learning or all about teaching? In my view, when every teacher finishes the classic mission statement starter-sentence, "We believe all students can learn . . ." with the statement, "and no student will fail on my watch," the school is most likely operating as a PLC.

The chapters that follow present a loosely structured set of professional learning sessions distilled from many years' work with teams—all designed to develop strong shared leadership between principals and teacher leaders. Use the suggestions as a customizable, flexible set of strategies that can be used in longer or shorter sessions to help your teacher leaders prepare to lead their colleagues in this exciting and critical work, enabling *all* students to achieve at the highest levels.

CAUTIONARY NOTES: WHAT IS YOUR LEVEL OF READINESS? ■

It is not too soon to discuss a few challenges that individual principals may face in sharing leadership. I believe any principal can learn to share leadership effectively, although some clearly find it difficult. I have seen that most aspects of leadership are learnable and all leadership can be constantly improved.

Opposite extremes can and do emerge when principals interact with teams of teacher leaders, even when one of the stated purposes of their work is developing shared leadership. At one end of the spectrum are extreme controllers. No meaningful work is accomplished, because the principal cannot relinquish control. One principal I observed simply never allowed the team's discussions to enter the realm of school-wide policies, practices, and procedures, and only at a very surface level addressed issues of curriculum, instruction, and assessment. Whenever a teacher tried to bring up something in an area of larger concern, he simply made a dismissive comment and moved the discussion back to something smaller and less significant. The teachers soon learned to keep quiet and let the principal do most of the talking—they knew their role was to agree with him.

Another principal set about working with her leadership team on a set of expectations for upcoming tasks for teacher collaborations. Historically, teams had been free to meet if they wanted, but there were no clear expectations about what to do if they did meet; or they could decide to use the time for individual teacher prep—as most did. After the work for the upcoming collaborations was rolled out to the staff, a couple of teachers went to her and complained. She reversed the team's decisions and allowed the time to revert to being used for whatever teachers wanted. It was obvious that she never regained credibility with her team.

Still another principal allowed her team to help design professional learning about PLC processes for the rest of the staff, but insisted on doing it all herself. When I privately suggested having a few of her teacher leaders co-present with her, which would have entailed helping them prepare their presentations, she balked and said, "They would never do it as well as I can." While I never saw her presentations, I was struck by the missed opportunity to create staff ownership of the initiatives. Even if the teacher leaders' segments were less than perfect, allowing and supporting their presentations would have made a huge symbolic statement of shared ownership—and most likely would have been the beginnings of increased ownership by the rest of the staff, whom the principal often complained were "very resistant."

One of the most extreme examples I have observed at the opposite end of the spectrum—abdication of leadership—also happened in a setting where the principal was interacting with the team as a whole. They had reached an important decision point, and there was dissention among the team members about how to resolve it. All the team was looking to the principal for guidance. At that point, she pulled away from the table and began texting on her BlackBerry. In amazement, I made my way over to her and asked in a whisper why she had left the group at this particular point. She said, "I want them to figure this out." It was a sadly misguided decision on her part. She let them continue to argue, and no decision was made. The team left that day in confusion about their work and their roles.

In another case, a first-year high school principal was named to a school whose leadership team was already attending bimonthly workshops to deepen their understanding and solidify their work in developing the school as a PLC. Deciding he had too many things to do as a new principal, he assigned the development of this team to one of the assistant principals (APs). The team, disheartened by the symbolic degrading of their work and believing that without the principal's firsthand involvement "this isn't going anywhere," their participation became politely superficial.

Both control and abdication are obviously wrong applications of the practice of shared leadership. Some principals seem to possess innate characteristics that make shared leadership a natural practice or next step for them, but I believe that self-awareness and conscious practice can improve these characteristics in any principal.

Principal Self-Assessment
for Shared Leadership Readiness

This is not a complete list, but here are some key traits for principals that make shared leadership easy—or, in absentia, more difficult. How self-aware are you? Rate yourself from 1 to 5 on these, just as you rated your potential GC members on the GC selection criteria:

Openness—Like the GC members I hope to choose, I remain open. As the leader, I do not possess all the answers. My teachers know more than I do about their content, and in many cases, about instructional practices that will best support their students in learning it. I have the bird's-eye-view of the school from my vantage point as principal, which they do not, but they have the detail about what is going on "on the ground." I do not have to have the final say on everything we should do to improve our school.
My self-rating: ____

Humility—I am learning, side-by-side, with my team. My positional authority does not allow me to send them off to learn without me. Although I am their boss, I do not behave in ways that show arrogance.
My self-rating: ____

Courage—I have overcome my fear that my teacher leaders won't do something exactly right. I allow them to make mistakes—always stepping in quickly with coaching questions to minimize any possible detriment to student learning.
My self-rating: ____

Empowerment—I do everything possible to develop teacher leaders whose leadership in certain areas could outshine my own. They might become (or are already) better presenters, facilitators, or askers of better guiding questions. In the meantime, they might not facilitate a process or present something as expertly as I can (or so I might think), but I am OK with that and affirm them for their work. I know when—and how—to give feedback that will help them grow, yet I am careful not to over-critique and make them fear they have to be perfect while they are learning.
My self-rating: ____

Judgment—I have the wisdom to know what I SHOULD be tight on. I know I cannot abdicate my role as the leader of the school, and the leader of the teacher leaders.
My self-rating: ____

Honesty—I never pretend to share decision making with my team when I have actually already made the decision or plan to make it. I know that nothing will erode my credibility—or this work—faster with my teacher leaders.
My self-rating: ____

Ideals and beliefs—I am tight on my beliefs about all students' ability to learn at the highest levels. I model respect for staff members even as I do not allow them or us to blame the students or parents for poor results.
My self-rating: ____

Self-reflection: Which of these do I need to spend more time reflecting on and improving my personal practice to share leadership effectively?

*****

What Does Shared Leadership Sound Like?

The idea of sharing leadership can be new—almost foreign—for some principals. In some cases, it helps to be able to begin to picture what it looks and sounds like before jumping in. Below are some sample statements that I have heard effective leaders make as they begin to move to a new style of sharing leadership:

FLEXIBILITY:

Right now, my thinking on this is _____. But my thinking could be changed. I'd like to hear from all of you.

SOLICITING INPUT FROM TEACHER EXPERTS:

As we look at our school data from the _____ assessment, I have some questions about the math data. _____, as a math person, what are your thoughts about the differences in the results for _____ students and for _____ students?

CLARITY:

We need to make a decision about _____. The only parameters I have for this decision are _____ and _____. Beyond that, we will make the decision as a team. Then I will inform the staff in the weekly bulletin, and then each of you can follow up with your own teams.

I have to make the decision about _____, and I will share my thinking with you about it. I am interested in your input, but I will be making the final decision.

EQUITY:

We haven't heard from _____ or _____ yet. Everyone's voice is important here, and everyone needs to weigh in on this.

What are some kinds of similar statements and/or questions you might begin to use as you begin to work with your GC in a new structure of shared leadership?

■ SUMMARY

It is impossible to overstate the importance of carving out structured time at regular intervals to meet with your guiding coalition; it is every bit as important as having time during the contract day for teacher teams to collaborate. Second, sharing leadership is a major departure from the way many principals lead, so I strongly urge you to take time to reflect on the self-assessment questions to ensure that you are ready to begin developing yourself—and your teacher leaders—to work together in new ways.

Access links and additional resources at
www.corwin.com/sharedleadership

3

Preparations

Your first meeting will set the tone for the development of shared leadership in your school.

A PERSONAL, IN-PERSON INVITATION BUILDS TRUST

How you go about the next step is crucial: It is of the utmost importance that you personally invite each of your selected team members to join the guiding coalition (GC) and attend the first and subsequent meetings. *This is not an invitation to be sent out in an e-mail or impersonally distributed into teachers' mailboxes.* Investing the time in speaking one to one with each teacher leader will yield a critical payoff: the foundation of a trusting relationship. This is important because you are breaking ground in a new area of shared leadership between yourself and your teacher leaders.

Teachers do not want to be invited to become administrators. And while many are open to rising as leaders, they may, paradoxically, be uncomfortable with being differentiated from their peers. This apparent contradiction is a residual effect of some schools' unfortunate history of a general lack of trust between teachers and administrators. Your initial, personal conversations are your first opportunity to delineate teacher leadership from administration and to reassure teacher leaders who may be hesitant that this important new role can be highly rewarding.

Each teacher leader on your GC will lead a grade-level or course-alike team. If you are a high school principal, this means you may have over 20 teachers on your GC. This represents a significant investment of your time in making personal invitations, even before you can hold your first meeting. I can only assure you that in my experience, every minute you spend upfront will pay important dividends. Trust must be earned.

So what do you say as you hold these conversations? Here is a possible conversation starter:

> As you know, some of us recently attended a conference about professional learning communities. We felt a lot of excitement as we learned about what this could do for our students. I want to get started before we lose that momentum. You are the teacher leader who came to mind first when I thought of who could best lead our [Algebra I team/second grade team]. I'm forming a new team I'm calling the guiding coalition to work with me to figure out how we are going to begin this work. I don't have all the answers—in fact, I feel like I don't have very many answers. I need teacher experts to lead this with me. Would you be willing to be a part of this?

If none of your teachers have heard of PLCs, or if you would rather avoid introducing another acronym at this point (see Chapter 1), simply begin your conversations with perceptual and/or numeric data:

> I've been listening to teachers' frustrations about how the students are doing, and as you know, we haven't had very good student results in the past [time frame]. I want to put some new structures in place to address that. We have teacher collaboration time already, but so many teachers are complaining that it's a waste of time, and that needs to change. We also need to revamp our [pyramid of interventions/Response to Intervention (RtI)]—something I need teacher expertise to figure out with me. I'm forming a new team I'm calling the guiding coalition . . . (see above).

Naturally, teachers will want to know what kind of time commitment is involved. Fortunately, you are prepared for this question because you have already sketched out a tentative calendar of meeting dates (Chapter 2)—to be finalized once the group is convened. If you are holding some of the meetings before or after work hours and paying the teacher leaders, share that information.

If one of your selected leaders is extremely hesitant, simply allow him or her time to think about it. He or she will undoubtedly want to know who else is going to be on the GC, so it will be helpful to first approach the teachers you think will be most willing, and have their yes answers secured as you move on to those who may be more hesitant.

■ PUBLISH THE INITIATIVE

Use your judgment about exactly when to go public about the convening of the GC. Remember, the natural grapevine of your school will begin to crackle with this latest development, and the old adage, "Whenever people don't have information, they just make it up" will hold true as ever. So don't wait too long. After you have a few yes answers, consider a concise bulletin, or ideally, an announcement at an all-staff meeting if you have one scheduled within a few days of your invitational conversations. This will be parallel to the one-to-one conversations—citing the data you have mentioned or the PLC conference you attended with some of the teachers, but addressed to the staff as a whole, letting everyone know that you are convening a team of teachers to share leadership with you to determine steps to move forward.

ESSENTIAL COMMUNICATION: DON'T LET YOUR PROMISING PLAN BECOME A NONSTARTER ■

As you begin inviting teachers to join your GC and informing the staff, keep your district supervisor in the loop, who can in turn keep the superintendent informed. In some cases, it is wise to hold this conversation even before you begin speaking to potential GC members. Particularly if teacher-administrative relations have been strained in the past, early fears about changing the status quo may generate alarms that are relayed to union leaders, parents, board members, and so on, especially if your school is the only one moving in this direction. Be sure to take as much private time as necessary with any teacher who raises concerns or comes to you for more information. Be transparent about why you have selected a new team that is different from the standing leadership team: this is a different kind of work and a different role for team members, that you are going to begin sharing leadership in new ways, and most important, that you need a small group to work with as you develop your own practice.

One way to allay fears—including possible nervousness on the part of potential GC members in your one-to-one conversations—is to label the initiative a pilot. Using this term conveys that it is a tryout, will develop over time, that the operational framework is not set in concrete, and that you expect bumps in the road that will be worked out. If you do this, however, be prepared to resist pressure to abandon the effort at the first bump—and be assured that there will be numerous bumps and glitches, as is the case with anything new. "But you said this was a pilot!" should not be a reason to stop the work. Instead, as issues arise, probe for understanding, and pledge to work out the glitches. Realize that something a teacher may feel is impossible—such as sharing her own students' work and data—is an essential step in the development of your school as a PLC. In flexible, loose-tight leadership, this is something you must be tight on— it is a nonnegotiable. However, teams' initial steps may be imperfect at first, so it is essential for them to get started and refine their procedures as they improve their teamwork. The leadership that is shared between yourself and the GC is essential to support this.

If you stop and consider the myriad initiatives you have watched come and go in your own school and district, it is obvious that most never reach a high level of implementation before they are cast by the wayside or simply fade away from lack of energy and attention. Douglas Reeves (2011) discusses the need for "deep implementation"—with 90% of the faculty implementing with 90% fidelity, 90% of the time. Timothy Waters and colleagues (2009a, 2009b, 2009), authors of the Balanced Leadership Program at Mid-Continent Research for Education and Learning (McREL), discuss the importance of Quality, Fidelity, Intensity, Consistency (QFIC) when implementing research-based practices. Teacher collaboration in a PLC is a key research-based practice. If you dub this work a pilot, deep implementation (with QFIC) over time is essential to ascertain its results.

An obvious question from teachers you did not select will be how you choose your team members. In a school with a history of negative regard for administrators by teachers, you may even hear allegations of favoritism. In my experience, the best answer is that you expect all teachers to be or become leaders, because schools with many teacher leaders get the best results for students, and since this kind of teacher leadership is a departure from tradition, you are going to work with a small group of teachers initially and expand to others over time—the ideal plan—and the teachers you have tapped for this pilot either have expressed interest in teacher leadership, or you simply had a sense that they would be open to trying a new role. However, do not be pushed into defining a specific time frame for GC expansion, because cultivating shared leadership is a developmental process and time lines vary considerably by school. But while you are developing your GC, watch for opportunities for other teachers to become leaders in different areas, especially those who are interested in becoming leaders and may be disappointed in not being chosen.

■ BLENDING TRADITIONAL AND NEW TEACHER LEADERSHIP

In schools where contractual time for teacher collaboration has already been instituted, some kind of procedure was used to assign team leader roles. Team leaders may be elected by peers, or the role may be rotated among team members annually (or even monthly!). The role may even carry contractual stipulations about selection, especially if they have stipends attached, as is typical with department chairs. At the secondary level, department meetings are a tradition that came with the bricks, but traditional department meetings are not conducive to the kind of collaboration that a PLC requires, especially if the school and its departments are large.

As a result, the department or grade-level team leaders now in place may not be the ideal candidates you identified in Chapter 2 for GC membership.

My best guidance is to allow some of the traditional duties to remain in place for the teachers in those positions, while your new team leaders begin to assume a different kind of role. For example, having department heads continue to order supplies and textbooks, make room assignments, and so on will probably not hinder the new work. A natural transition is to move other responsibilities such as responsibility for agendas and team minutes to GC members, because these will take on different forms than in the past. At the secondary level, be fully transparent with the possibility that course-alike team meetings are likely to gradually replace department meetings.

At the elementary level, if the grade level chair currently in place is not a GC member, consider the kinds of duties that the grade level chair can continue to fulfill outside of grade level collaboration time, since the use of that time will be changing. Then at the end of the year, month, or whatever term the traditional grade level chair role expires, transition the role of team leadership solely to GC members.

PREPARING FOR THE FIRST ◼
MEETING OF THE GUIDING COALITION

You have now spoken personally to each teacher leader you have selected for the GC and invited them all to the first of your regularly scheduled meetings. What is the time frame for this meeting? Ideally, it should be longer to lay the groundwork for subsequent meetings, which may be held at other times, such as during a common prep or before or after school. I recommend allowing 3 to 4 hours for the first meeting. After you read through the Agenda Notes, you may even decide to allocate a full day, depending on your own background and that of your team.

One purpose of GC meetings is to model effective meeting practices. Thus, it will be strong modeling to send out the agenda, which follows, in advance.

What is described here may seem ambitious for a single meeting. If the agenda feels unrealistic for your time frame and/or the team you have selected (who, after all, have never operated as a team before), simply break the agenda into smaller chunks to be addressed over several meetings. As you use this guidebook, remember that no two schools are alike. Feel free to customize the suggested sequence as well as the learning activities to meet the needs of your team and your own developing leadership style. You are learning to more effectively share leadership, while your teacher leaders are ramping up their leadership skills for working with colleagues in a new way.

In preparing suggested materials and equipment for GC meetings, consider providing a blend of hard copy and electronic formats to accommodate the preferences of various members and to prevent feelings of being burdened with a new set of "stuff" to keep track of. Less technology-inclined members will appreciate receiving a binder, with handouts for each meeting already three-hole punched when they arrive. More technology-inclined members will appreciate having documents sent out electronically in advance so that they can access them on their own devices during the meeting. Consider providing each member with a flash drive to facilitate document sharing, storage, and backup. Many companies selling promotional products offer personalized flash drives that can be customized with your school name or logo—a small token of your appreciation for the teacher leaders who are willing to embark on the shared leadership journey with you.

HOW TO USE THE AGENDAS ◼

The agendas reflect a typical—although flexible—sequence of professional learning I use with school teams. In my work, certain agenda items become standard for all subsequent meetings. I have found that modeling this consistency benefits teacher leaders and increases their confidence in facilitating their own teams. Teacher collaboration may be new in some schools. In others, collaboration may lack structure, often leading to complaints that it is a waste of time. At worst, some teams may be dysfunctional, presenting a challenge for all members. The litmus test of teacher collaboration is this: Are student outcomes continuously improving as a result? If not, introducing and maintaining routine structures is a very reliable path to supporting teacher leaders to raise the bar for their teams.

As principal, you are facilitating professional learning for your teacher leaders, while simultaneously developing yourself as a shared leadership principal. For principals with less experience in planning and facilitating professional learning, detailed facilitation notes may be found on the companion website. As you use this book, feel free to customize your own agendas and the sequence of GC meeting topics so that they make sense for your own school's development as a PLC.

I invite principals at all levels to consider and try out the suggested tools in the agendas. Some leaders—both administrators and teacher leaders—sometimes fear reactions to any tool that formalizes teachers' team meetings. Initial complaints may range from "too artificial" to "too elementary" (from secondary educators) to "this is just dumb" or "too weird." My guidance is always something like, "Just try it. Let it be weird—it's OK." Current team reality may be that the focus is not really on student learning or quickly wanders afield. The intent is to bridge the gap between less-than-effective or less-than-efficient meetings to highly focused meetings where the planned tasks are accomplished efficiently. The goal is continuously improving student learning. Keep returning to that intent. Rest assured that each graphic organizer, strategy, or other tool you will encounter has been used by countless school teams at the high school, middle school, and elementary levels. If graphics such as clip art are problematic, delete them—some high school teachers disengage when they see clip art, assuming they are being presented with something designed for elementary teachers. Know your teachers and adjust accordingly. One high school administrative leader said,

> Really like the rotating roles, and ensuring everyone on the GC has experience as the leader/facilitator . . . that also would have helped me enormously, if as a teacher I had to do that, not only to be better prepared if I ever went into admin, but also just to be more self-confident as a teacher among my colleagues, whether I ever went into admin or not. Also, when it is "required"—"we're all going to experience all of the roles"—it eliminates the self-consciousness associated with "oh, but I'm not a leader . . . but I'd like to be . . . but I'd probably be embarrassed so I'm not going to try . . ."

Your teacher leaders deserve all the support you can give them to gain confidence in leading their peers, and that is exactly what the tools are designed to do. So as you consider and select the tools you will introduce, also be willing to step out of your own comfort zone so that you can push in the right places—for students!

■ OPTIONS FOR PLANNING

As you come to each agenda's Team Planning step, your team always has a couple of options. One is for the team leaders individually to take the new routines back to their teams and introduce them. Another is for you and GC members to present and facilitate them with the whole staff together as they sit by teams in a staff meeting or professional learning session. If your team chooses the latter route, it is critical that you *and* some of the GC members co-facilitate. This represents leadership solidarity to the staff—essential for supporting your teacher leaders. GC members should rotate the co-facilitation roles if that is the chosen option so that over time all members are symbolically presented as leaders. An advantage of the latter option is that this will give GC members with challenging teammates an increased level of confidence leading the new routines for the first time with their teams in this semi-public setting. Meanwhile, you will be on hand to rotate among teams, helping troubleshoot and clarify. Then as a full group wrap-up, you will state the expectations and time line for teams to embed the new routines into their meetings during regular collaboration time.

All that said, in schools with a strong, positive culture with most staff open and willing to grow professionally for the benefit of students, having GC members introduce the routines on their own works fine, and can result in moving all of the work ahead at an accelerated pace, given the removal of the need to always have to wait for the next staff meeting.

ONE MORE CAUTION ■

Please don't use PowerPoints for your GC meetings. I thought twice before adding this section. It's almost as drastic as asking participants to turn off their personal devices and physically put them away in a meeting, because people who love PowerPoint, well, they love it. So if you do, before you abandon this book, please hear me out.

PowerPoint is a presentation tool and good one. I use it often in a variety of settings, although not usually for small groups. The concerns I invite you to consider about using PowerPoint for your GC meetings include:

1.   PowerPoint and similar presentation tools set up a presenter-audience dynamic that is, by its very nature, contrary to what you are attempting to create with your teacher leaders. As soon as you launch your PowerPoint, symbolically, as the presenter, you are the expert and they are the learners. All your messages about developing *shared* leadership and figuring things out together suddenly have the legs cut out from under them.

2.   It is likely that at this beginning point in your shared leadership journey to develop your school as a PLC, you don't have all the answers. There is something about launching that presentation that implies that you do. While you want your teacher leaders to have confidence in your ability to lead this work as the Learning Leader, you also want to convey an attitude of being the Lead Learner, and to me there is a difference. The Lead Learner—while still in charge, still accountable for virtually everything that goes on at the school—is, in this setting, a partner, learning shoulder-to-shoulder with the teacher leaders. Shared leadership is grounded in shared learning.

3.   I like PowerPoint sometimes because it can help me stay the course in a fairly certain sequence of activities and discussions that I have carefully planned, knowing the audience and setting well enough to be confident that I will execute it all with—probably—a minimum of surprises. Unfortunately, I have seen too many PowerPoint users who have become

enslaved to the notion that they must finish the PowerPoint no matter what is going on with the human beings in their sessions. In these instances, its use actually seems to contribute to a certain rigidity in thinking on the part of the presenter. It creates a barrier between the presenter and the audience; the ability and/or willingness to read and respond to audience cues is diminished because the presentation has taken over. It happens so often, I don't think it's a coincidence. In your setting, much of what may occur in a GC meeting is unplanned and unanticipated, and it is critical that you are able to be ultra-responsive. Yes, you have a time constraint, and a planned agenda. But if you can suspend your usual habit, and try holding these meetings without PowerPoints, I think you will be amazed at your own flexibility, and the reserves of responses and ideas that you didn't realize you had; your teacher leaders will find themselves freed up from being watchers and learners to become active creators, taking ownership of the work. The absence of a PowerPoint will be immediately noticed and will serve as an important symbol that you are embarking on a new journey together—the journey of shared leadership.

4.   Preparing a PowerPoint adds yet another dimension of time-demand to preparing for your GC meetings. You probably have enough to do already.

(Note: if you and the GC members decide to use staff meetings or full staff professional learning sessions to introduce new team routines to the faculty as a whole, I'm not suggesting that you shouldn't use PowerPoint in that setting.)

■ SUMMARY

Trust is foundational to shared leadership. Begin with a *personal, in-person* invitation to your chosen teacher leaders to join the guiding coalition (GC). Communicate your intent and plans to your district supervisor early in the process, and time the publication of the initiative to the full staff as soon as possible after you have gotten a few yes answers to your invitation. Use the suggestions in this chapter to prepare thoroughly for the first GC meeting. The agendas are not intended to be prescriptive, so use them as a guide, especially if you are experienced and comfortable planning and facilitating professional learning.

 Access links and additional resources at
www.corwin.com/sharedleadership

4

Guiding Coalition Meeting— Getting Started

This critical meeting grounds the work of the guiding coalition in the tenets of professional learning communities (PLCs). It will clarify school-wide roles now that the guiding coalition has been formed. It will also introduce numerous tools for use in future GC meetings, as well as for GC teacher leaders to use as they lead their own teams.

Agenda

Guiding Coalition Meeting

1. Welcome and Thank You
   - Parking Lot and Talking Stick

2. PLC—Definition

3. School-Wide Roles
   - Principal
   - GC Members
   - Department Chairs/Grade-Level Chairs

4. Rotating Meeting Roles/Responsibilities

5. Norms

6. Team Planning

7. Tool Kit

8. Evaluate Norms

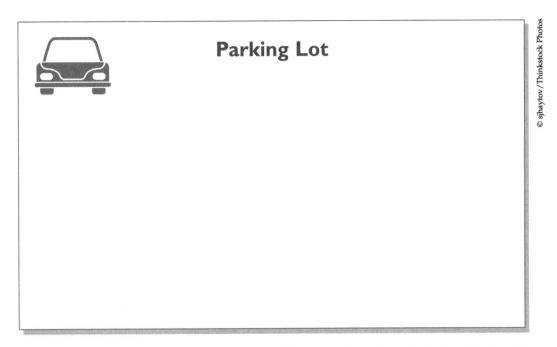

Parking Lot

The Talking Stick

The talking stick tradition comes from various Native American tribes, with these ritual objects used in tribal councils to signify the right to speak and be heard by all. According to Dr. Carol Locust (n.d.) of the Native American Research and Training Center, "When matters of great concern came before the council, the leading elder would hold the talking stick and begin the discussion. When he finished what he had to say he would hold out the talking stick, and whoever wished to speak after him would take it. In this manner the stick was passed from one individual to another until all who wished to speak had done so."

Locust also writes, "The speaker should not forget that he carries within himself a sacred spark of the Great Spirit, and therefore he is Iso sacred. If he feels he cannot honor the talking stick with his words, he should refrain from speaking so he will not dishonor himself. When he is again in control of his words, the stick will be returned to him."

In the work of teams, the talking stick is passed respectfully hand-to-hand and is never tossed or thrown. Since only the person holding the talking stick has the

right to speak, and anyone wishing to respond must patiently wait for the stick to be passed to him or her, the use of this symbolic object serves to slow down and potentially disarm very contentious discussions. The protocol of passing the stick from hand to hand helps break down the potential for arguments and increases the likelihood that members of the team really listen to each other, mentally processing the words that were just spoken. It also helps ensure that quieter or shy members have the opportunity to speak and diminishes the probability that any one member will dominate. Teams that become accustomed to using the talking stick for important discussions find that the equity it provides for all members makes it a valuable tool.

What Is a Professional Learning Community (PLC)?

"An ongoing process in which educators work collaboratively in recurring cycles of collective inquiry and action research to achieve better results for the students they serve" (DuFour, DuFour, Eaker, & Many, 2010).

Notes:

Questions of a PLC

1. What do we want the students to know?

2. How will we set them up for success?

3. How will we know when the students have mastered the learning?

4. What will we do when some students do not learn?

5. What will we do for students who have already mastered the learning we are planning?

Adapted from DuFour and DuFour (2012), p. 26.

Notes:

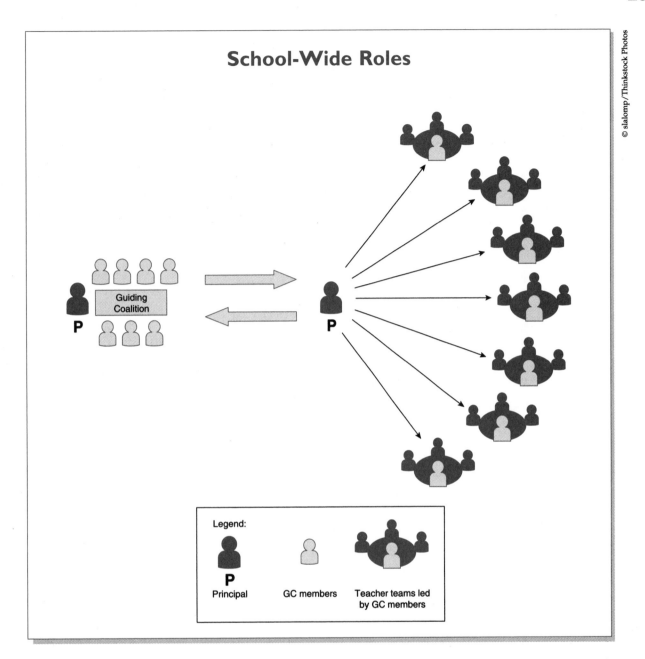

School-Wide Roles

Legend:

P — Principal

GC members

Teacher teams led by GC members

Role Tent Cards

Developed by Judy Cunningham, Cunningham
Associates; Used With Permission

Facilitator

- Adheres to group norms
- Clarifies role of group
- Keeps group on task
- Directs processes
- Encourages everyone to participate
- Asks for clarity when needed
- Protects participants and ideas from attack
- Contributes to group task
- Remains neutral to the content

Facilitator

- Adheres to group norms
- Clarifies role of group
- Keeps group on task
- Directs processes
- Encourages everyone to participate
- Asks for clarity when needed
- Protects participants and ideas from attack
- Contributes to group task
- Remains neutral to the content

Developed by Judy Cunningham, Cunningham
Associates; Used With Permission

© slalomp/Thinkstock Photos

Developed by Judy Cunningham, Cunningham
Associates; Used With Permission

Timekeeper

- Adheres to group norms
- Contributes to the group task
- Monitors adherence to time limits

Timekeeper

- Adheres to group norms
- Contributes to the group task
- Monitors adherence to time limits

Developed by Judy Cunningham, Cunningham
Associates; Used With Permission

Developed by Judy Cunningham, Cunningham
Associates; Used With Permission

Spokesperson

- Adheres to group norms
- Contributes to the group task
- Keeps notes if needed
- Summarizes the results to others in the room

Spokesperson

- Adheres to group norms
- Contributes to the group task
- Keeps notes if needed
- Summarizes the results to others in the room

Developed by Judy Cunningham, Cunningham
Associates; Used With Permission

Developed by Judy Cunningham, Cunningham
Associates; Used With Permission

Norms Monitor

- Posts the norms
- Reviews the team norms
  at the beginning of the meeting
- Uses signal (previously decided by the team)
  to indicate need to work within the norms

Norms Monitor

- Posts the norms
- Reviews the team norms
  at the beginning of the meeting
- Uses signal (previously decided by the team)
  to indicate need to work within the norms

Developed by Judy Cunningham, Cunningham
Associates; Used With Permission

© Dutchicon/Thinkstock Photos

Developed by Judy Cunningham, Cunningham Associates; Used With Permission

• *Recorder*
• Supports facilitator
• Contributes to the group task
• Charts basic ideas
• Asks group what not to record
• Uses earth tone colors
• Writes legibly
• Transcribes charted notes afterward and distributes to all team members and the administrator

Recorder

- Supports facilitator
- Contributes to the group task
- Charts basic ideas
- Asks group what not to record
- Uses earth tone colors
- Writes legibly
- Transcribes charted notes afterward and distributes to all team members and the administrator

Developed by Judy Cunningham, Cunningham Associates; Used With Permission

© Ieremy/Thinkstock Photos

Developed by Judy Cunningham, Cunningham
Associates; Used With Permission

Engaged Team Members

- Adheres to group norms
- Contributes to the group task
- Listens to others
- Opens the door for others to speak

© sialomp/Thinkstock Photos

Engaged Team Members

- Adheres to group norms
- Contributes to the group task
- Listens to others
- Opens the door for others to speak

Developed by Judy Cunningham, Cunningham
Associates; Used With Permission

Developed by Judy Cunningham, Cunningham
Associates; Used With Permission

- **SMART(e) Goal**

- **Action Plan**   *(10 min.)*

- **Solutions**   *(brainstorm 10 min.)*

- **Challenges**   *(5 min.)*

- **Successes**   *(5 min.)*

- **Successes**   *(5 min.)*

- **Challenges**   *(5 min.)*

- **Solutions**   *(brainstorm 10 min.)*

- **Action Plan**   *(10 min.)*

- **SMART(e) Goal**

Developed by Judy Cunningham, Cunningham
Associates; Used With Permission

Our Team Compact

Eighth-Grade English
Team

- Arrive prepared and on time

- Stay focused

- Assume positive intentions

- Disagree agreeably

- Balance advocacy and inquiry

How will we remind each other of our norms?
Each team member will have a Norm face, which we will display when someone begins to violate a norm.

Five Steps to Effective Norms

1. Develop—All members develop norms together, record on chart/poster, and sign when finished

2. Post—Poster displayed in meeting area, and/or norms listed on each printed agenda

3. Review—Facilitator reviews (reads) norms at beginning of each meeting

4. Remind—Visual or audio signal when someone is beginning to violate a norm

5. Evaluate—2 to 3 minutes at the end of every meeting, including discussion about any norm that was not followed consistently

Professional Work Plan and Team Commitments

_____ to _____
(Today's Date)   (Next Meeting Date)

Focus of our work for this period: _____

School-Wide Actions With Staff as a Whole
Principal actions for whole-staff communication, support, and implementation:
GC members' actions to support whole-staff communication and implementation:

(Continued)

(Continued)

Tools we will use: _____

TEAM-LEVEL ACTIONS FOR THIS PERIOD

GC members' individual plans for team meetings to implement what we've learned:

Team _____   Team meeting date/s _____

Team _____   Team meeting date/s _____

Team _____   Team meeting date/s _____

Team _____   Team meeting date/s _____

Team _____   Team meeting date/s _____

Team _____   Team meeting date/s _____

Team _____   Team meeting date/s _____

Team _____   Team meeting date/s _____

Team _____   Team meeting date/s _____

Suggested Materials and Equipment for Agenda

- Handouts, three-hole punched
  - Agenda
  - Talking Stick background
  - What Is a Professional Learning Community (PLC)?
  - Questions of a PLC
  - School-Wide Roles
    - Roles/Responsibilities Tent Cards*
    - 1 set of 7 tent cards for use in GC meetings
    - 1 additional set of 7 for each GC member
    - Additional Engaged Team member tent cards for GC meetings and for teacher leaders to use with teams
  - Team Compact (Sample norms)
  - Five Steps to Effective Norms
  - Professional Work Plan and Team Commitments for individual note taking, as desired
  - Tool Kit
- Chart rack and blank chart paper, markers
- Binders and/or flash drives
- Poster size copy of agenda posted (or projected)
- Questions of a PLC enlarged to poster size
- Professional Work Plan and Team Commitments enlarged to poster size, including additional copies of page 2 to include all teams
- Poster size copy of Tool Kit
- Parking Lot enlarged to poster size and hung in the meeting area
- Sticky notes, 3x3 inches or larger for potential Parking Lot items
- Object to serve as a Talking Stick

*Cards are best made by duplicating on card stock, then cutting apart and folding. It is helpful to make enough additional Engaged Team member cards to include the rest of the GC, after the roles of Facilitator (principal), Timekeeper, and Recorder have been filled. Consider making additional Engaged Team member cards for GC members to use as needed in their own teams. The SMARTe card is simply a team reminder that goal setting includes *every* student.

■ AGENDA NOTES

Parking Lot

If a discussion point arises that will be likely to take more time than the agenda allows, or an issue comes to mind that is not on the agenda, it is recorded on a sticky note and put on the Parking Lot. It is then addressed at the end of the meeting if time allows, at the next meeting, or dealt with in some fashion between meetings.

Talking Stick

A Talking Stick is not used for every discussion, but at any point where it is important for each voice to be heard, it may be introduced. Team leaders can introduce it whenever one or more members are dominating while others are not speaking up. It is especially useful when a topic is likely to be contentious, because passing it slows down the interchange.

The Talking Stick is passed respectfully from hand to hand and is never tossed or thrown. Sometimes the facilitator may ask for each member to weigh in on some question or issue, and the talking stick is simply passed in order of seating around the circle. While anyone may pass, use of the Talking Stick encourages those who usually do not speak up to take the floor when it reaches them. Thus, introducing and using the Talking Stick during teacher collaboration gives teacher leaders another helpful tool.

PLC Definition

Key concepts

1. PLC refers to the culture of an entire school.

2. The purpose of, and reason for becoming, a PLC is to ensure that all students in the school succeed at the highest levels. When teachers work individually and in isolation, student success is at risk.

3. The work of teachers in a school that is a PLC is driven by the Questions of a PLC.

What a PLC is not:

1. A meeting

2. A team of teachers

Clarity on the PLC term will help prevent misunderstandings as the work commences. Statements like, "Our PLC starts at 2:00 on Thursdays," or "Maria and John are in my PLC" illustrate misunderstandings of the term.

Questions of a PLC

Each time a team plans a new unit of study these questions should guide the planning for the specific skills and knowledge of the unit.

Question 1 refers to the team's identification of the highest-leverage skills and knowledge for focus in the unit, from the most enduring, high-leverage, and essential skills they have identified in the curriculum for the year.

Question 2 refers to scaffolding, pre-teaching, and other, individualized support to ensure that English Learners, students with disabilities, and any students who are underprepared will be able to succeed.

Question 3 refers to methods of assessment and criteria for mastery.

Question 4 refers to the reteaching loop (which may be missing in some classrooms), especially how this will take place within the team, given pacing guides and other time constraints.

Question 5 is an important planning question, which assumes that some students will have already mastered the knowledge and skills and need to extend their knowledge and/or have enrichment experiences so that their learning time is not wasted.

If the school's culture has historically been characterized by most teachers routinely teaching everything whole group, the Questions of a PLC may cause concern. Be prepared with a few "back pocket" responses. Here are some messages that may help assuage early fears:

- When teachers begin to work collaboratively to plan instruction, all the students become the team's responsibility.
- The collective expertise of every team is superior to individual expertise.
- Collectively planning scaffolding and pre-teaching will benefit the students of everyone in the team.
- Within each team, teachers can potentially regroup students at any time for pre-teaching, reteaching, and enrichment/extension.
- Collaborative planning will begin moving us toward failing fewer students and having all students be successful.
- We are working in stages for our school to become a PLC. This is a process.

Be mindful of your school's history of teacher teams. In some schools, teaming is viewed as a way to divvy up the work. In other words, "I'll plan Unit 1, you plan Unit 2, etc., and as a team we'll all share." This is not how teachers collaborate in a PLC because the elements of group thinking and team planning are missing.

Or perhaps some teams already enjoy sharing favorite activities and suggested materials and equipment. While sharing and collegiality are certainly desirable, these alone do not define PLC collaboration. What is missing here is critical discussion about the activities and suggested materials and equipment, asking, "What is the *best* lesson sequence and student learning experience/activity to ensure that all students will achieve mastery as we have defined it?" Sometimes, a favorite activity may actually be extraneous to the essential learning the team has defined in Question 1.

While none of the Questions of a PLC directly target *how* individual teachers will instruct the essential learning, the purpose of collaboration is for each teacher to optimize his or her instruction so that all students will be successful. Teachers have individual styles, and working as a PLC does not mean that all the teachers become cookie cutter copies of each other. The intent is that *variability in the essential curriculum that every student receives* is reduced or eliminated. This is the only reliable way to ensure equity for all students.

That said, certain instructional strategies trump others for producing student learning within the essential curriculum, and teachers have a professional responsibility to use those that are most effective. Once students have completed the assessment (Questions of a PLC #3), team members compare results to see what kind of instruction was most successful for the most students, then apply those discoveries as they plan the next unit.

Robert Marzano (2003) coined the term "guaranteed and viable curriculum." Curriculum is *guaranteed* if every student—regardless of teacher—receives it. It is *viable* if it can be taught to mastery during the instructional time available during the school year. DuFour (2015) provides an extensive discussion about the ostensibly "narrowed" curriculum of the Common Core State Standards (CCSS), including a detailed example (of how it has not been narrowed) from fourth-grade language arts CCSS, taken from *Leaders of Learning: How District, School, and Classroom Leaders Improve Student Achievement* by DuFour and Marzano (2011). In short, the CCSS are still not, by this definition, viable for U.S. schools, so Question #1 entails critical discussions in teams—on an annual basis for pre-planning and pacing, and during regular collaboration throughout the year—to prioritize and focus their instruction on the highest-leverage, most enduring and essential skills and knowledge.

School-Wide Roles

The intents behind forming a guiding coalition include leadership, communication, and decision making. GC meetings will focus on just-in-time leadership discussions related to team meetings that members will be leading in the next few weeks. The two-way arrows in the handout represent two-way communication. Since GC members represent the entire teaching staff, input may be gathered during GC meetings related to various decisions.

In a shared leadership school, decisions fall into several categories. Some—mostly operational decisions—are made by the principal or administrative team. For others, GC input is asked prior to an administrative decision. A third category of decisions are made by the GC and principal in tandem. The intent is not to involve GC members in administrivia. The team's valuable time is devoted to issues of curriculum, instruction, and assessment within the context of the Questions of a PLC.

GC members are responsible to keep their own team members informed of decisions, solicit input formally from time to time, and lead collaborative team meetings to accomplish specific tasks.

In the early stages of shared leadership, the principal facilitates GC meetings. In time, GC members who are willing begin co-facilitating or take over facilitating.

The principal regularly drops in on teacher team collaborations and is available as needed to work with GC members as they work with their teams in a leadership role.

Rotating Meeting Roles/Responsibilities

Designated Roles/Responsibilities support high-efficiency meetings, especially the roles of Facilitator and Timekeeper. Using the cards is helpful for teams because it supports members' learning and consciously practicing the various roles. Ideally, roles and responsibilities rotate from meeting to meeting, except that the Facilitator role will always fall to the GC members as they lead their own teams, and for GC meetings, for now, to the principal. On very small teams some roles may not be needed. A Recorder may be needed occasionally, and a Spokesperson when teams meet in a full-staff setting. There is a Monitor role but it is more effective if all members monitor norms (addressed in Agenda Item 5). If the Norms Monitor role is used it should rotate from meeting to meeting. The SMARTe planning card can be set aside for future meetings, when teams have become familiar with that specific agenda protocol.

For the best introduction of Roles/Responsibilities, invite volunteers to be Timekeeper and Recorder for the rest of the day's GC meeting. Distribute additional Engaged Team Member cards to everyone else. Set a time frame for the Timekeeper to use—for example, every 20 minutes—for reminding the group of how much time remains.

Norms

In my experience, the vast majority of issues that teacher leaders encounter in leading colleagues can be prevented and/or respectfully addressed by a thoughtful process of developing norms, coupled with the use of all four of the other Steps to Effective Norms. There are many methods for developing group norms, and it is important for the GC to develop its own Team Compact, as well as one or more agreed-upon signals in case someone begins to violate a norm. See on the companion website for a possible facilitation strategy for this agenda item. I suggest having each member sign the final poster.

Having a Norms poster on the wall is essentially useless in the absence of the other steps. Here are some examples of reminder signals (Step 4):

Natomas High School's Leadership Team (Sacramento, CA) cut out a picture of the face of Norm (from the old TV series *Cheers*), duplicated it, and mounted the faces on Popsicle sticks. When anyone began to violate a norm, group members held up Norm's face.

Brookside Elementary's Instructional Leadership Council (Beaumont, CA) would chant, "Ribbit. Ribbit. Ribbit" when someone began to violate a norm. The school's mascot was The Bullfrog.

The Algebra I Team at Moreno Valley High School (Moreno Valley, CA) agreed on a different nonverbal signal for each norm. For example, if someone came in late, the rest of the team would begin tapping their watches or wrists. If sidebars developed, other team members would signal the basketball T (timeout) sign. If someone said something disparaging or disrespectful, the rest of the team would give that member the "shame on you" finger rub.

A common objection to norm reminders is that they are dumb or childish. Unfortunately, without reminders, norms are merely hopeful suggestions. Invite team members to simply try out a given reminder or set of reminders for a period of time. Reminders can be changed, but having them is essential for norms to have value.

Team Planning

A key element of each GC meeting is team planning. In shared leadership, building shared knowledge is essential and will be part of each GC meeting. But then what will be the plan for the teacher leaders to share and implement it with colleagues?

The Professional Work Plan and Team Commitments is a tool to guide team planning. As discussed in Chapter 3, there are always a couple of options for this plan. One is for each GC member to introduce new concepts and routines to the team he or she leads. The other is to introduce them to the whole staff at once, with the teachers sitting by teams. Either way, you will need to support your teacher leaders with an explicit statement to the staff of agreed-upon expectations for all teams. For example, the GC may agree that following this meeting, teams will

- implement the Five Steps to Effective Norms by a specific deadline set by the GC,
- begin using the rotating Meeting Roles/Responsibilities,
- begin using a Parking Lot to keep meetings on track, and
- begin using the Questions of a PLC as a basis for team discussions.

Consistency of expectations helps prevent objections such as, "Why is our team the only one that has to have norms?" Introducing as-needed tools such as the Talking Stick also supports team leaders. In the case of the Talking Stick, although it is not used in every meeting or in every discussion, it is valuable for contentious topics or on teams with members who have developed a habit of dominating discussions.

Tool Kit

Shared leadership represents a major departure from the hierarchical, top-down structure of a traditional school. As GC members begin to assume leadership roles that differ from past practice, keeping a running list of the tools they can use—both in a group memory (chart) format and individually—supports their success in the transition. For example, in this GC meeting, tools have included using a posted agenda (sent in advance), the Parking Lot, the Talking Stick, Questions of a PLC, Norms/Five Steps to Effective Norms, Member Roles/Responsibilities, and the Professional Work Plan and Team Commitments form.

Evaluate Norms

Ironically, this is the part of the agenda that is easiest to shortchange or simply skip. Yet it is so critical that without it, teams—even the GC—may quickly begin to disregard the norms they spent valuable collaboration time developing. Effective leadership is essentially influence. Your teacher leaders do not have positional authority over their team members, but providing tools helps strengthen their influence. This step appears on every agenda in this book, and I urge you to provide strong modeling for your teacher leaders by taking the time for it at the end of every meeting.

Only a few minutes is needed to evaluate norms. A simple method is to go through each of the newly agreed-upon norms and ask team members to indicate with a "fist to five" (fist indicating zero, five being the highest) how well they felt each norm was followed. Invite discussion about any disagreements in ratings. If you feel a rating is inflated, call attention to it.

You might say something like, "I don't think I agree that we were a five on number two. I would maybe give us a three, since we had several sidebars today. What do you think?" After any discussion ask, "What would help us in the future?" The obvious answer to this question is to use the agreed-upon Norm Reminder. Ask for group commitment to work on any norm that was weakly adhered to (e.g., "Do we have everyone's commitment to work on this one next time?").

Adjournment

If there were items placed on the Parking Lot, address these as time allows. If time is up, consider whether the item(s) can be handled in some way between now and the next meeting. If not, be sure to place the item(s) on the next meeting agenda.

Of course, be sure to thank GC members for their time and their commitment to this important work for students. Reaffirm your own commitment to supporting them, including being available for one-to-one conversations about concerns that may arise.

■ AFTER THE MEETING— PRINCIPAL FOLLOW UP SUGGESTIONS

1. Send a thank you e-mail to GC members for attending, including a reminder of the next GC meeting date and time.

2. If the team chose to have each member take back the new concepts and routines to their teams individually, send a short all-staff memo outlining the expectations for the upcoming month's team collaborations: norm development, including reminder strategies, time devoted to discussion of What Is a PLC and the evolving roles for staff, and practice using the rotating Meeting Roles/Responsibilities. Regardless of the option chosen for launching new team practices, each time the GC meets, teachers will be curious about what was decided and what is coming next. Keeping the whole staff informed as the process of developing shared leadership unfolds will be crucial to success, thus preventing the rumor mill from undermining the work. So even if the plan is to use full-staff professional learning, I strongly recommend sending a *brief* meeting summary to all teaching and support staff as soon as possible after the GC meeting. Develop the habit of sending out timely summaries in this way, and they will come to be expected. This will smooth the way for staff to more easily accept the changes that are planned.

3. If posters need to be removed from the meeting room, assign an office staff member to take charge of these until the next meeting, as well as the Roles/Responsibilities tent cards.

4. Reflect (consider beginning a journal or a private blog on your computer for these leadership reflections): What was successful about this meeting? What concerns do I have? Which team leader(s) may need increased support from me? What red flags should I watch for in the next several weeks?

5. In your personal calendar, enter your schedule of visitations for team collaborations. How long will you sit in on each meeting? Is any team a priority, based on what you have just learned in your first GC meeting?

6. Take whatever actions are possible to address leftover Parking Lot issues, or add them to the next meeting agenda.

TROUBLESHOOTING ■

The initial weeks may be bumpy in the transition from whatever the status quo has been for teacher collaboration (including none) to expectations for more highly structured team meetings.

At the secondary level, if teachers have been used to attending only traditional department meetings, the new structure of course-alike teams will probably feel uncomfortable to some. These are much smaller teams; there is nowhere to hide, and some teachers may already be expressing concerns about new expectations, which, they may fear, could mean more work and are probably yet to be fully defined.

At the elementary level, it may be that, until now, grade level teams have had a lot of autonomy about how they spend collaboration time. Some may not even meet, or may just meet for a few minutes, then go off to their own rooms again to work in isolation. In other schools, teams may meet, have a formal agenda, and submit minutes to the administrator, yet nothing of significance is happening to improve instruction individually or collectively. The teachers may be collegial—even friendly toward each other. They may share suggested materials and equipment or even divide up work tasks such as designing activities for upcoming units. However, the Questions of a PLC do not drive the discussions. One superintendent terms these meetings "tea and cookies," and they can occur at the elementary, middle, or high school level.

Expect some resistance. Check in frequently with team leaders, because they will encounter peer resistance in many forms and in a variety of settings, including and outside of team meetings. Know your individual leaders' level of confidence and ability to work with different personalities, and be prepared to balance your leadership as needed between stepping up (restating expectations, holding private conversations with resistors) and stepping back (coaching team leaders to work with resistors on their own). Both are important. It is essential for the staff to know what the principal will insist on. Otherwise, the teacher leaders will be left highly vulnerable, since they do not have positional authority to require colleagues to do anything. But as time goes on, coaching the GC members to work with their own resistors builds their confidence and skill. Solid peer leadership, shared by the GC with the principal, is ultimately more powerful and much more effective than administrative directives. However, your courage and willingness to respectfully and appropriately deliver a directive to a resistor may be essential in the beginning. In *Cultures Built to Last: Systemic PLCs at Work*, Richard DuFour and Michael Fullan (2013) write:

> The most powerful form of accountability in a loose-tight culture is peer-to-peer accountability, rather than traditional top-down supervision. But ironically, the only way to develop lateral accountability

is for leaders to demonstrate a willingness to address the situation when people do not honor core values and practices. In high-trust schools and districts, leaders are more—not less—likely to confront those who demonstrate a lack of commitment to their students and their colleagues. (pp. 58–59)

■ SUMMARY

The first meeting of the guiding coalition provides the foundation for shared leadership in a professional learning community (PLC) by introducing/ reviewing school-wide roles, responsibilities, and the Questions of a PLC as the touchstone for how teams utilize their limited and valuable collaboration time. This agenda also launches key tools and routines for members to introduce to their own teams. Their consistent use during GC meetings will support team leaders in overcoming discomfort and developing confidence using them. Initially, some of the tools and routines may feel artificial— hence the potential discomfort. Traditional ways of operating schools as hierarchical structures are as disarmingly comfortable as they are ineffective for improving school-wide learning. Despite their seeming artificiality, if you and your teacher leaders are open to trying and perfecting new tools and routines such as those suggested in the agendas, they significantly accelerate the progress of teams in moving from "meetings as usual" to high-level collaboration for the improvement of outcomes for all students.

 Access links and additional resources at
www.corwin.com/sharedleadership

5

Essential Learnings and Common Assessments

Before considering the next meeting agenda for the guiding coalition, the topics of essential learnings and common assessments merit some reflection. These are at the heart of teacher collaboration in a PLC, but because of the complexities, and varying places schools and teams may be in their development, it is wise to step back and view them from a birds-eye perspective in your school.

Whether your state and/or district has transitioned to Common Core State Standards (CCSS) or has opted out, your students are likely assessed annually using some high-stakes test based on agreed-upon content standards. Smaller, formative assessments are becoming more widely used during the instructional year. If these are in place, these more frequent (i.e., monthly), smaller common assessments may be logical places for teams to begin collaborating.

In the past, teams in many schools were expected to analyze and discuss end-of-year and/or quarterly state- and district-level assessment results. However, depending on their frequency (for district benchmarks), and the turnaround time for access to the results, these discussions were often more of an autopsy than an opportunity to assess immediate learning and instructional effectiveness. This is not to say that discussing larger common assessments does not have value from a wider, programmatic standpoint, but if teams are to devote precious collaboration time to analyzing them, there should be a strong focus on evaluating the effectiveness of specific aspects of their instructional program for students, especially since it is probably too late to catch those who showed that they were falling through the cracks.

■ QUESTIONS OF A PLC—QUESTION #1

Teams must complete an annual map of their curriculum as a first step to answering Question #1, unit by unit. As discussed in Chapter 4, even if your school and/or district has transitioned to CCSS, the curriculum has not been narrowed enough to be viable for the time your teachers have for instruction. Richard DuFour (2015) suggests these simple steps for teacher teams to create annual curriculum maps of standards that are enduring, essential, and high-leverage:

1. All members are provided with a copy of the following for the team's grade level or course.

    a. The Common Core State Standards or standards unique to their state

    b. The district curriculum guide

    c. A "wish list" of skills from the grade level or course above theirs that articulates the three or four key skills entering students should have to succeed at that level

2. After discussing their findings, each team posts three pieces of butcher paper on the wall with the headings "Keep," "Drop," and "Create."

3. Each member is then given three different colored sticky notes—yellow for Keep, pink for Drop, and green for Create—and asked to assess the significance of each standard.

4. The team considers each standard, and each member is asked to place it in one of the three categories.

5. When the team has completed its task, it presents its findings to the teachers in the grade levels above and below its own to seek feedback and look for redundancy.

6. The team establishes a pacing calendar that stipulates the sequencing of the content and the amount of time that will be devoted to each unit. Note that this pacing calendar will not be prescriptive, as in, "We must all be on page 20 by Tuesday." It will indicate the skills and concepts to be taught in a particular unit and the length of the unit. Day-to-day decisions about instruction are left to the judgment of each teacher.

Source: DuFour, R. (2015). *In praise of American educators and how they can become even better*. Bloomington, IN: Solution Tree. Used with permission.

PURPOSES OF TEACHER ■
COLLABORATION IN A PLC

Effective teacher collaboration in a PLC has several specific outcomes:

- Identifying the most essential, enduring, high-leverage standards as the focus of the year's curriculum, and in turn for each unit of instruction.
- Creating or selecting assessments/assignments to determine whether students have mastered the learning for the unit.
- Catching students at risk of failing for the purpose of planning improved scaffolding and pre-teaching, as well as providing an immediate reteaching loop if necessary.
- Planning ways to regroup students within the team for these purposes as needed (more on this in Chapters 14 and 15 on interventions).
- If a student needs a just-in-time intervention that the team cannot provide, determining where it can be accessed in the school's Pyramid of Interventions and/or Response to Intervention (RTI).
- Previewing upcoming instruction and planning improved instructional strategies for continuously increasing student success. In Chapter 15, the agenda for the GC meeting will address the school's Pyramid of Interventions or RTI. Unfortunately, an often-missed point is that a Pyramid of Interventions cannot overcome the lack of best first instruction. Best first instruction at the classroom level constitutes the *base* of the pyramid.
- Designing extension and/or enrichment learning for students who have already mastered what is about to be taught.
- Looking ahead at future topics to decide whether the originally planned instructional time to be allocated is adequate, too generous, or even unnecessary.
- Using the Questions of a PLC to keep the focus on student learning. This includes keeping the needs of high achieving students—often the most neglected learners—in mind as instruction is planned. Increased focus on improved instruction for the neediest students is essential to close achievement gaps, but it is easy to forget that those who are gifted and high achieving have needs as well. I would argue that these students have always been somewhat neglected; a tendency to "teach to the middle" is not new. During collaboration, effective teams examine all the PLC Questions, including "What will we do for students who have already mastered the learning we are planning?"

THE ROLE OF TRUST ■

For teams that have only experienced "collaboration lite," the notion of everyone's sharing and discussing their student-by-student results with team peers can be daunting. Historically, teachers' private practice has thrived in U.S. schools, to the detriment of students.

This can be approached in stages for teams that are not ready for full disclosure. While all team members need to receive their own results as well as the results for each of the other teachers, the results can initially be distributed without teacher names or class designations, but with each teacher having his or her own class results individually (privately) marked. This is more work for the team leader, but it may be a necessary stage for teams that are new to collaboration. Over time, as trust develops and relationships are strengthened, team members will realize that there is not only more efficiency but also more value—and no threat—to openly sharing results teacher by teacher.

A good reminder is that the end purpose of collaboration is improving the students' learning, not critiquing or comparing teachers' performance.

■ WHAT THE RESULTS REVEAL

As trust develops, team members are able to set aside personal fears and egos and compare student results. The results will reveal which instruction was most successful with the most students. It is important to look at the results student by student, because it is likely that not all classes on the team have a similar makeup. Students may be clustered with specific teachers based on individual education plans (IEPs), stages of English acquisition, or gifted identification. For discussion purposes, these designations should be indicated in each class roster's presentation of results.

■ THE IMPORTANCE OF TARGETING

In my experience, teams who get maximum value for their students from collaboration develop short, common assessments such as quizzes, performance tasks, and/or common assignments of varying kinds, which can all serve as effective formative assessments of learning. The key is that they are targeted—the team decides exactly which essential, enduring, high-leverage skill or competency each common measure will assess. It is obviously not possible to collaborate about every nuance of the curriculum, even after teams have completed their annual plans to reduce the sprawling real estate ostensibly covered by the curriculum most schools purport to deliver by mapping out the most essential, enduring, high-leverage skills and concepts they will teach for the year. The frequency and time frame for teacher collaborations also factor into these decisions. Teams who meet weekly can develop and discuss assessments on skills and competencies that are much more incremental than teams who meet monthly, for example.

In addition, although a team may regularly administer a common large-scale test or longer quiz, they will gain more traction by selecting a targeted set of related items for collaboration or may even decide to reduce the scope of the assessments. In one case, the Algebra I team at Moreno Valley High School in Moreno Valley, California, was already giving a common weekly quiz. However, the teachers realized that the quiz was too long and included too many kinds of items to demonstrate student learning on the most essential concept of the week. In the end, they began developing a three-item quiz for the weekly assessment, with the three items targeting a particular concept but varied in complexity and difficulty. This enabled their discussions of student learning to zero in on specific students' struggles and to evaluate the effectiveness of their instruction much more accurately.

ASSESSING ESSENTIAL ■
LEARNINGS: IT DOESN'T HAVE TO BE A "TEST"

Teams miss valuable opportunities to monitor the pulse of student learning when they think of collaboration only in terms of tests and quizzes. Common assignments and performance tasks have at least equal value in light of the goals of teacher collaboration discussed above. This is not to say that every assignment, performance task, quiz, or test has to be common across the team, but the selection or development of those that will be discussed during collaboration should be based on high-leverage, targeted skills and competencies, which the team has agreed are essential for student success in the overall course as well as the next course.

THE NEED TO SEEK ■
OUT IMPROVED STRATEGIES

When a team analyzes the results of small, frequent, common assignments, performance tasks, or short, targeted assessments such as quizzes student by student, it is not unusual for them to realize that no one on the team possesses the knowledge of a strategy, or set of strategies, that is needed to sufficiently meet student needs. This will be apparent from the results.

When that is the case, specific team members take on the responsibility of investigating other sources of expertise—teachers in other grade levels or departments, teachers in other schools, experts housed at the district office, and resources from print and the Internet. Occasionally, outside conferences and training can be valuable if they are focused on exactly what the team needs, but it can be easy to overlook resources that are close at hand, which should be researched first.

EXAMINATION OF PAPERS, ■
PRODUCTS, AND PERFORMANCES

An unfortunate tendency in team collaboration—even among sophisticated teams—is to look only at numerical score data. Thus, they miss the opportunity to see specifically what kind of errors students are making, how they are working out their thinking on paper, and even what behaviors they engage in while learning and demonstrating learning, which can be captured in video clips. By bringing the student papers and products to the collaboration, discussions are more meaningful and more useful for planning and intervention.

At the secondary level, the most practical approach is for each team member to bring a sampling of papers that are exemplars of students who were successful, those who just missed the learning objective, and those who missed the boat completely. For teachers of performance-based classes such as PE and performing arts, video clips—assessed with rubrics and checklists—are the ideal work samples for team examination. And in virtually any classroom or subject area, video clips also offer valuable glimpses into student thinking and learning behaviors.

■ THE JAPANESE LESSON STUDY STRUCTURE

Using this structure, teachers select an upcoming, in-depth student competency for collaboration. They collectively plan a lesson—which everyone will eventually teach—with one teacher volunteering to have the rest of the team observe her students while she delivers it. A critical feature is that team members focus their observations on the students, not the teacher. The team meets immediately afterward to discuss their observation notes and examine the student work. They use this information to plan an improved lesson, and another teacher volunteers to teach it publicly for the team, followed by another group debrief. If time allows, a third, improved lesson may be planned and delivered for the team by a third volunteer. Depending on the curriculum pacing, non-volunteers may wait until these cycles are completed before teaching the lesson themselves, or they may have already taught the collectively planned lesson, and simply share their own observations with the team.

Clearly, unless a team has mapped out its essential curriculum for the year, finding this much time to spend on any particular lesson is a challenge. After having completed their annual curriculum map, teams that want to experiment with the Japanese model might elect to try it once per quarter or once per semester with a lesson of particular importance. It is an example of collaboration at a very powerful, highly professional level.

A very good resource for background on Japanese lesson study and how-tos for beginning teams is *Lesson Study Step by Step: How Teacher Learning Communities Improve Instruction* by Catherine Lewis and Jacqueline Hurd (2011).

■ A WORD ABOUT VERTICAL TEAMS OR TEAMS OF SPECIALISTS

In very small schools, teacher teams may span multiple grade levels, and at the secondary level, singletons—teachers who are the only ones teaching their set of courses (e.g., band, ceramics, and other specialized courses)—may comprise a team such as "Enhancement Subjects" or "Specialists Team." Of course, if electronic collaboration or driving to a central location to collaborate with colleagues of like courses is possible, that is ideal. Unfortunately, it is not always feasible on a regular basis. Thus, collaboration in these vertical or specialized teams must be different from that of course-alike teams to be meaningful. Since common assessments are not possible, other forms of discussion protocols are needed for these teams to have collaborations that are useful for all the purposes outlined at the beginning of this chapter. One of these, the Student Work Protocol, will be presented in Chapter 10. It is still necessary for teachers on teams like these to become comfortable sharing their own students' work and their lessons that produced it, and then allowing the rest of the team to offer their best thinking and feedback to help each teacher continuously improve student learning.

MOVING COLLABORATION TO THE NEXT LEVEL THROUGH SHARED LEADERSHIP ◼

So where are your teams at this point? What is your best next step to work with the teacher leaders of the guiding coalition to move collaboration to the next level?

The agenda for the next GC meeting will include a survey designed to help your GC teacher leaders calibrate where their teams are right now on the collaboration continuum.

SUMMARY ◼

Robert Marzano's (2003) research on effective schools identified a guaranteed and viable curriculum (GVC) as a factor having a significant impact on student achievement; indeed, the highest of the 11 factors identified in that meta-analysis. But a GVC is impossible without teams' identification of essential learnings so that common assessments can be developed. Assuming that common standards result in a GVC is a mistake; even the Common Core State Standards have not been narrowed enough to ensure a GVC. Tests and quizzes are only one way for teachers to assess essential learnings, and teams should fully utilize a range of assessment strategies so that improved instructional approaches can be designed.

Access links and additional resources at
www.corwin.com/sharedleadership

6

Guiding
Coalition Meeting

*More Best Practice
Meeting Routines, Essential
Learnings, and Common Assessments*

This guiding coalition (GC) meeting builds on the best practice meeting routines of the first meeting, with the addition of Community Building and the After Action Review (AAR). The AAR is an invaluable tool to help the GC share responsibility with you for monitoring and supporting the work of all teams. During the AAR, each GC member will share team products as they are developed by his or her team. This will provide opportunities for the guiding coalition to celebrate successes, trouble-shoot, and generally support each member to lead their individual teams in developing high quality products according to agreed-upon timelines.

This meeting will also introduce, in the team setting, the topics of essential learnings and common assessments—the heart of teacher collaboration in a PLC, as discussed in Chapter 5.

Beginning with this meeting, each agenda will follow a consistent format, with new items shown on the agenda in highlighted text.

I encourage principals to use this book as a guide—customizing the agendas, the sequence of topics, and facilitation plans. I also encourage the practice of consistently including routine items on each GC meeting agenda. The elements that become routine will assist GC members as they lead their colleagues, enabling them to confidently use the same routines as they lead collaboration in their own teams.

■ THE CASE FOR ROUTINE STRUCTURES: DISRUPTING OLD PATTERNS

While there is nothing particularly remarkable about the tools and routines presented in these agendas, each tool was designed to meet a need, fill a gap, or address an issue that is common in schools at all levels when teachers are first expected to get into teams and begin collaborating. As discussed in the Introduction, nothing in traditional teacher preparation programs prepares teachers to lead colleagues. Further, teacher isolation is so ingrained in many U.S. public schools that it amounts to a sacred cow. In spite of the many benefits of collaboration for teachers—although the proven outcome of effective collaboration is the benefit to students—initial resistance is quite common, given what some teachers perceive as the loss of personal autonomy, fear of having weaknesses exposed, and/or the fear of an increased workload. Remember that initial attempts at meaningful collaboration may be bumpy. That is why having teacher leaders internalize these kinds of tools and routines is so valuable. How does this help? They *disrupt the typical patterns of interaction* that may have come to be accepted and cemented in place when teams meet, and/or they lay the foundation for prevention, much as a strong teacher, who has instituted well-designed classroom routines for students, reduces the opportunities for discipline problems to arise. This is certainly not to equate teachers with students, but there are certain parallels in group behaviors that routines can ameliorate. Routines help create a safe, predictable environment.

This is not to say that the possibility of resistance or unprofessional behavior is eliminated. But having these tools and routines to fall back on gives the teacher leaders leverage if they do.

■ PREPARATION FOR THE GC MEETING

Send meeting reminders to GC members, and ask them to bring copies of their team norms. Tool Kit handouts will be used and added to in each meeting.

Suggested Meeting Setup:

- Post the Questions of a PLC for reference
- Post the signed Norms poster

Agenda

Guiding Coalition Meeting

1. Review Norms and Assign Meeting Roles

2. Community Building

3. After Action Review

4. Collaboration Survey

5. Team Planning

6. Tool Kit

7. Evaluate Norms

After-Action Review

Date _____

After Action Review for _____ (Team)

What We Set Out to Do	What We Did

What Worked	What Didn't

What We Learned	Next Steps

Collaboration Survey
for Course-Alike Teams

1. My team discusses a common assignment, performance task, quiz, or test at least once (a) _____ .

    Week   Semimonthly   Monthly   Quarterly   Annually   Never

    Using a scale of 1–6, with 6 being the highest, circle your rating for the following items:

2. My team routinely focuses our discussions on the Questions of a PLC.

    6   5   4   3   2   1

3. My team shares and examines student results student-by-student, teacher-by-teacher.

    6   5   4   3   2   1

4. In each collaboration, my team discusses a highly targeted set of items (or a performance) that assess(es) student learning on an essential, enduring, high-leverage skill, skill set, or competency.

    6   5   4   3   2   1

5. My team routinely examines student work—papers, products, performances (e.g., video clips) to augment numeric scores.

    6   5   4   3   2   1

6. Team members routinely ask each other to describe the strategies they used to attain strong student learning, based on teacher-by-teacher results, and these strategies are incorporated by all members in plans for upcoming instruction.

    6   5   4   3   2   1

7. My team is comfortable with members' visiting each other during instruction.

    6   5   4   3   2   1

8. We regard all the students in our team as "our students."

    6   5   4   3   2   1

9. My team routinely seeks out other resources for instructional strategies when none of our members had strong student success on the common assignment/assessment/performance task.

    6   5   4   3   2   1

10. My team routinely identifies students at risk of failing and collaboratively designs interventions/reteaching loops, as well as scaffolding and pre-teaching strategies for students who need them.

    6   5   4   3   2   1

11. My team routinely previews upcoming instruction, selects or designs common assessments to measure the most essential, enduring, high-leverage skills and competencies, and agrees on strategies we all will try with our students.

    6   5   4   3   2   1

12. My team's student results are steadily improving.

    6   5   4   3   2   1

Collaboration Survey

for Vertical Teams or Teams of Specialists

1. Each member of my team presents an assignment, performance task, quiz, or test at least once (a) _____.

   Week   Semimonthly   Monthly   Quarterly   Annually   Never

   Using a scale of 1–6, with 6 being the highest, circle your rating for the following items:

2. My team routinely focuses our discussions on the Questions of a PLC.

   6   5   4   3   2   1

3. On a rotating basis, each member of my team shares student work, and its data as applicable (rubric scores, assignment/quiz scores, checklists, anecdotal data, etc.), for the purpose of team feedback.

   6   5   4   3   2   1

4. Team members routinely ask each other to describe the strategies they used to attain strong student learning, and these strategies are incorporated by other members in plans for their upcoming instruction as appropriate.

   6   5   4   3   2   1

5. My team is comfortable with members' visiting each other during instruction.

   6   5   4   3   2   1

6. We regard all the students in our team as "our students."

   6   5   4   3   2   1

7. My team routinely seeks out other resources for instructional strategies to augment members' suggestions to each other.

   6   5   4   3   2   1

8. My team members routinely help each other identify students at risk of failing and collaboratively brainstorm and suggest interventions/reteaching loops, as well as scaffolding and pre-teaching strategies for students who need them.

   6   5   4   3   2   1

9. My team members routinely share previews of upcoming instruction, including their planned assessments to measure the most essential, enduring, high-leverage skills and competencies.

   6   5   4   3   2   1

10. My team's student results are steadily improving.

    6   5   4   3   2   1

Suggested Materials and Equipment for Agenda

- Handouts, three-hole punched
  - Agenda
  - After Action Review
  - Collaboration Survey for Course-Alike Teams
  - Collaboration Survey for Vertical Teams or Teams of Specialists (if applicable)
  - Professional Work Plan and Team Commitments for individual note taking, as desired

- 1 poster size enlargement of each survey to be used
- Signed Norms poster
- Roles/Responsibilities tent cards
- After Action Review enlarged to poster size
- Chart rack, markers, tape
- Talking Stick
- Poster size copy of agenda posted (or projected)
- Questions of a PLC enlarged to poster size
- Professional Work Plan and Team Commitments enlarged to poster size, including additional copies of page 2 to include all teams
- Parking Lot enlarged to poster size and hung in the meeting area
- Sticky notes, 3x3 inches or larger for potential Parking Lot items
- Mini Avery dots—use a single color (avoid yellow, which is hard to see)—precut the sheets of dots into sets of 13 dots each for team members
- Tool Kit poster with notes begun in last meeting

■ AGENDA NOTES

Review Norms and Assign Meeting Roles

This meeting is your first opportunity to begin consistently modeling the use of these routines.

Community Building

Community building is a best practice for meetings because, gradually, team members come to know each other better both personally and professionally. Over time, community building helps forge personal relationships, which people come to value and care about protecting; impacting, in a positive way, how they behave toward each other. This raises the likelihood that the team will operate in an increasingly collaborative fashion, characterized by courtesy, respect, and openness to each other's ideas.

Unfortunately, meeting facilitators often tend to skip community building because it may be seen as a "fluffy" activity that simply takes time (these are sometimes referred to as *icebreakers*). In reality, it can take just a few minutes and is an investment with significant payoffs in helping teams work more smoothly. Community building also sets a positive tone for the meeting, which is especially important in times of high stress, or if there have been recent negative developments that are impacting team members.

Community building not only can be a consistent, routine procedure such as Good News, but can also take a variety of other forms and be more elaborate if time allows. Community builders can also be designed to focus the group on the main topic of the meeting, which is a very effective opener with a large group, such as a whole staff.

For this meeting agenda, I suggest using Good News. Share a brief Good News item of your own first. Good News can always be either personal or professional. I recommend sharing a personal family item, but it could also be positive information about something that has recently happened at school that some of or all the team members may not have heard. After your own Good News item, encourage anyone who wants to volunteer a Good News item to share it with the team. Continue until everyone who chooses to share has done so.

After Action Review

Using an AAR enables the team to see what is working and what is not and provides reminders of items that should be carried over into the new Professional Work Plan. I suggest using the poster-size form for the team (or it may be projected and typed into). Individual members may use the AAR handouts to take notes if they wish.

It works well for the Timekeeper to time the five AAR sections at 5 minutes apiece, with a 1 minute warning if needed. The Recorder can chart the group's work. As Facilitator, you decide whether to allot a specific number of additional minutes to any given section if you feel it is valuable, but continue to ask the Timekeeper to time it. Although AAR discussions are always valuable, it is easy to spend so much time on this activity that the rest of the agenda is shortchanged. What We Did will need additional time for a large guiding coalition, such as at a high school, because that is the segment where each teacher leader will share his or her team products developed since the last GC meeting.

What We Set Out to Do is based on the Professional Work Plan of the last meeting. It typically requires less than 5 minutes.

What We Did may differ from the Plan for a variety of reasons, most commonly, time constraints. This section is divided into What Worked and What Didn't, to help the team regroup and make an improved Professional Work Plan next time. For this meeting, be sure to allow each GC member time to share the norms his or her team developed. Also include discussion of new tools members have tried out with their teams, such as talking sticks, role cards, and the Parking Lot.

What We Learned is probably the most important section of the AAR. Allotting a couple of extra minutes to this section can be valuable if new insights are emerging.

Next Steps are notes about what is needed in relation to revisiting parts of or building on the last Professional Work Plan. These may be folded into today's new plan, along with actions related to the new content of today's meeting.

After the AAR is completed, if the meeting space allows, move the poster off the chart rack to the wall space so that it can be referred to as the new Professional Work Plan is developed.

Collaboration Surveys

These surveys describe the work of high-functioning collaborative teams. It is unlikely that all items will be highly rated by all team leaders. You may wish to draw on the material in Chapter 5 to set the context for the team before using the surveys.

I suggest having each teacher leader on the GC complete the appropriate survey privately, then using the Avery mini-dots on the poster-size surveys to create a profile of teams school-wide. After the team has had time to consider and discuss the range and commonalities of collaboration across the school, it is helpful for the Recorder to begin capturing the group's ideas and agreements on chart paper. The Talking Stick can always be introduced to ensure that all voices are heard. See the companion website for discussion questions that may be used to debrief the surveys, including discussions of time frames for teams to move their collaboration discussions to a higher level around student performance.

Consensus Building

Whenever the Talking Stick is used it is fairly easy to tell when you have attained consensus. However, if the discussion bogs down as it moves to agreements for all teams, you may wish to introduce the fist-to-five strategy for consensus building.

You might begin by saying: We are moving toward consensus, so let's take a poll of where we all are. A fist means zero, or total disagreement, and a five means total agreement. Please hold up your fist-to-five position at this point in our discussion.

For those with a fist-to-two or less, ask: [Robin], you are showing a [one] on this agreement. What would it take to get you to at least a two?

Allow that member to express his or her concerns, then continue the group discussion to try to address them or reach a compromise. Continue with that member until a three is reached. Repeat with any other member at a fist-to-two and continue until everyone on the team is at least at a three.

Your concluding statements might go something like this: We are now between a three and five, which means we have consensus. We may still have specific questions or issues to work out, but consensus means that everyone here will support this agreement when we leave this room, both privately and publicly to everyone else outside this group. Consensus is much stronger than voting, because those who voted against something and lost can always say that they didn't vote for it. That is why in our teams and on our staff we will no longer vote on issues unless we have an outside mandate to take a vote. Fist-to-five is a strategy you can begin using right away as you lead your own teams. *(Note: If you did not need to use fist-to-five to gain consensus on the agreements you just made, you may still wish to introduce it if time allows, because it is such a valuable tool for leaders.)*

Save the notes captured by the Recorder for team planning.

Tool Kit

GC members—and the Recorder—may add the following items to their individual and the team's Tool Kit: Community Building, After Action Reviews, use of surveys, Avery dot strategy for group surveys, fist-to-five consensus building (if introduced).

AFTER THE MEETING— ■
PRINCIPAL FOLLOW UP SUGGESTIONS

Most of the Principal Follow Up notes from the end of Chapter 4 apply here. Principal Follow Up Item #4 is to Reflect. Although any current or former principal knows what a challenge it is to find a few private moments to reflect, I highly encourage you to close your door and take 5 to 10 minutes to journal, jot notes in a notepad or private blog, or simply think back over the meeting you just facilitated. Think about successes or glitches, next steps, what went as you expected, and anything unexpected that occurred. What are you learning about your teacher leaders, and what are you learning about yourself as you move along the path to increasingly shared leadership? Are you comfortable, confident, and (especially) consistent in communicating what expectations you will be loose on and what you will be tight on? Have you communicated this well to the GC? Your teacher leaders are counting on this as they take new risks as the leaders of their teams.

Consider the team products that were shared at this meeting. Did all the team leaders bring their team's norms? If some did not, what support do they need? Be sure to prioritize those teams for your upcoming visits during collaboration. With all teams you visit, depending on when you are present, note whether norms are posted and reviewed at the beginning of the meeting, whether team members have a signal to remind each other when norms are not being followed, and how the team evaluates their norms at the end of the meeting. Also note whether any teams need to add a norm to address a specific behavior or issue.

An ex-military colleague of mine was fond of saying, "No plan survives execution." There are myriad reasons for this, ranging from pushback from resistors, to overloaded To Do lists. On that note, one challenge of using Action Plans is ensuring that everyone who has an assigned task will remember to complete it—including yourself! If it becomes clear that this is a problem with you and your team, consider appointing a Task Reminder. The role of the Task Reminder is to check in with those who agreed to take on tasks in the Action Plan, reminding them to help ensure these are being done. Usually, one reminder is sufficient, possibly with an additional last minute check-in before the next GC meeting, or before a full staff professional learning if that is what the GC has planned. This is probably the kind of thing your office manager is good at, but it is more logical—and reinforces your commitment to shared leadership—to have a GC member assume this role.

■ TROUBLESHOOTING

Even more than after the first GC meeting, feelings of concern on the part of the teacher leaders, and fears and push-back from other staff members, may be evident in the days following this meeting, while GC members begin communicating with their teams about the next steps in the work of using common assessments and moving collaboration to the next level.

As the practices of common assessments and sharing of student work develop, teams will begin to experience new insights about their instruction and their students, and breakthroughs in their ability to work as a true team. Be prepared to celebrate small and large wins! Being a cheerleader for your teams, and especially for your teacher leaders, is a key function you need to fill in these early stages. This behavior was termed *affirmation*—one of the 21 Leadership Responsibilities of effective principals identified in the research of Marzano, Waters, and McNulty (2005), which was the basis of *School Leadership That Works: From Research to Results*.

Continue to balance your leadership between stepping up into a more directive role and stepping back into being more of a coach and guide. Your teacher leaders will develop leadership muscle as you coach them through rough spots in leading their teams, but in other instances it is equally important for you to step up and work privately with negaholics and resistors. Remember that moving from private practice to meaningful collaboration represents a major upheaval for some teachers. Small steps and stages are acceptable and often necessary; unprofessional behavior and pressure to wait forever to get everyone on board are not. Take whatever time is needed to clarify, restate expectations, and communicate—to any and all staff, often and well. Make this work your priority. So much of a principal's time is spent putting out operational fires—what Stephen R. Covey (1989, 2004) termed "the urgent," which can eternally eclipse "the important." Keep prioritizing the all-important "people work" as you move your school along the road to becoming a PLC through shared leadership.

■ SUMMARY

This GC meeting introduces additional tools and routines and makes use of a Collaboration Survey to assess where each team is operating in identifying essential learnings and using common assessments, and then to plan next steps. Since schools vary widely—as do teams within a given school—each team leader should come out of this meeting with next steps specific to his or her team, while you will be prepared to communicate the agreed-upon expectations to the staff as a whole.

Access links and additional resources at
www.corwin.com/sharedleadership

7

Guiding Coalition Meeting

Mission, Vision, Collective Commitments

Y ou may be wondering why this chapter and this guiding coalition (GC) meeting are located here instead of at the very front of the book. While the placement may seem counterintuitive, it is based on my years of experience working with school teams. In 2002, I became Administrator of the Riverside County School Leadership Center of the California School Leadership Academy (CSLA), a statewide network providing professional development for new and aspiring administrators and school leadership teams. At that time, the Vision module was one of the first in the program series for both school teams and individual leaders. I continued using CSLA's sequence after converting the program to align with PLC principles when CSLA was defunded by the state of California, making the first team session focused on Mission and Vision.

What I eventually came to realize was that this was really not what teams needed first. Instead, they needed a clear understanding of the new roles of teacher leaders who share leadership with the principal—a role that is still not clearly defined in many schools and districts—along with concrete tools for working with their teams of colleagues at the beginning stages. Revisiting the school mission and developing their vision did not come at the right place in teams' hierarchy of beginning needs. Another issue was that while it seemed that Mission and Vision were somewhat esoteric and abstract for this early stage, when what teacher leaders wanted and needed most were practical tools, some teams—and principals—could get so sidetracked by and enamored with Mission and Vision that it could become a comfortable detour from the initial, harder work. I found that Mission and Vision became much more meaningful when I placed them just a little later in the series, after teams had had some practice with foundational, best-practice meeting routines and a lot of conversation within their site teams about their new roles.

That said, one can also argue the merits of having the Mission and Vision solidly in place and/or refined ahead of time to provide rationale for a new kind of teacher leadership, for embarking on the PLC journey, and to be used as a first line of defense when push-back occurs. I certainly acknowledge that argument and will say again that this book is designed as a guide, not a bible, and that if you feel strongly about addressing Mission and Vision first in your sequence of work with your guiding coalition, you should definitely do so.

■ REFINING THE MISSION

Two schools of thought about refining (or writing) your mission statement can be summed up as follows:

1. "Just take ten minutes and knock that sucker out!" (This is author and speaker Dr. Robert Eaker talking—if you have ever been lucky enough to hear him speak on the topic of mission statements, you will probably remember this advice.)

2. The mission statement belongs to all stakeholders, so we should engage them all in an in-depth process when we write or refine it.

Be warned that the second school of thought can keep you on the Mission Statement Mission for a very long time. Remember that the first approach can still include a variety of stakeholders. Personally, I recommend either Dr. Eaker's approach, or some tweener of the two. Ideally, the mission statement should be concise but capture the highest aspirations the school has for its students. Well-written mission statements can provide a metric, which, in a global sense, can be used to measure the worth and congruence of possible courses of action. For example, if an elementary school is considering joining Advancement Via Individual Determination (AVID) so that more high-poverty students and their families will begin to consider the concept of college now instead of later, its members can refer to the school's mission to see if that decision is a fit. Likewise when the fifth-grade team approaches the principal with a proposal for an expensive conference.

Your mission statement captures your school's purpose. What is its reason for existing? What if all the parents in your school's attendance area had other choices? Why would they choose your school? A strong mission statement is concise. It is free of weasel words and phrases—such as "students reaching their highest potential"—that place reduced responsibility on the educators, and fit comfortably with traditional school operations and norms, such as teacher isolation and autonomy. Traditional mission statements often include poetic phrases such as "creating lifelong learners." While there is nothing wrong with including such phrases, they have little immediacy (not to mention zero measurability) compared to aspirations that are more urgent and targeted, such as "all students performing at or above grade level." The latter assumes that the educators in the school have the expertise to fulfill the mission and/or are fully committed to doing whatever it takes to fulfill it through a continuous cycle of collaboration and collective inquiry. A powerful mission statement continuously spurs action.

DEVELOPING THE VISION   ■

When Loretta Houston became principal of Grant Elementary in the Riverside Unified School District, California's Standardized Testing and Reporting (STAR) system had just been launched. Grant's scores came in 27th out of the 28 district elementary schools. This came as no surprise to anyone. The school served some of the poorest students in the district. The school plant itself, built in 1935, was in sad disrepair. When the custodian found a window broken, he simply boarded it up and did not put in a work order for glass replacement "because it will just get broken again." Teachers were working hard but in large part believed that since their students had the deck so strongly stacked against them, there wasn't much the school could do to improve their scholastic performance, and the STAR scores just came as another piece of bad news.

Loretta tackled Grant's problems on many fronts, deciding right away that shared leadership was essential to make any headway. She brought a team of teacher leaders to the CSLA School Leadership Teams program and included her office manager—an unusual move, but one that Loretta felt was important to build ownership of the school's future with all staff members. During the session on Vision, each school team was asked to design a cover for *Time* magazine featuring their school. What would the headline say? What sidebar stories would the feature article include? Grant's team decided that their headline would read, "Grant Elementary Named Distinguished School for the Fifth Time!" To understand how audacious this team's vision was, in addition to having just come in next to last in the first round of STAR assessments, the school had four homeless and rehab shelters in its attendance area, the third highest poverty level and the highest transiency rate in the district. To become a California Distinguished School, a school had to meet the most rigorous criteria in a range of areas. To even begin the extensive application, a school had to have STAR scores—an Academic Performance Index (API)—in the 700s, and Grant had just scored 519.

Fast forward 4 years. I could see Grant Elementary School from my office window. For the longest time it had had a playground that was mostly dirt; grass had only been planted fairly recently in the playing fields. I knew nothing about the school aside from its appearance, but understanding where it sat in Riverside, I was impressed when it appeared on my list of California Distinguished School Recognition Program (CDSRP) Validation Visits. One of the many hats I wore during my years in an area service agency was county lead for this state program, and at that time, most of the schools in the county that attained the recognition—or even qualified to apply—were those serving middle and higher income students.

When I went to the school and met with the school's leadership team, they provided all the required documentation for the validation visit, which we discussed in excruciating detail as per the CDSRP validation require-ments, along with conducting classroom and campus walk-throughs. Near the end of the document discussion, someone placed a rolled up chart on the table. When it was unrolled, it turned out to be the *Time Magazine Cover Story*. I recognized it right away because I was familiar with the exercise, although I had not been part of CSLA when Grant's team participated in the program. Someone explained that when the team returned from the Vision session, they had hung the poster in the staff room. It had remained there for the past 4 years, as teachers had moved from isolation to collaboration; from having no skills in collecting, using, and sharing classroom data to becoming data experts and using SMARTe goals (see Chapter 13 for a definition); and from instructional practices that hit loosely toward the middle of the class to highly targeted instruction on state standards using research-based practices. The school had improved more than 200 API points in 4 years, and achieve-ment gaps were rapidly closing. Teams were engaged in sophisticated collab-oration that had dramatically changed classroom practice. If the district had not closed its smallest elementary schools, including Grant, when the Great Recession hit, I have no doubt that Grant Elementary would have gone on to repeatedly achieve the California Distinguished School recognitions as the first leadership team envisioned. However, it is not the recognition based on qualifying test scores that is important in Grant's story, although such an affir-mation is certainly a boon to any school community. Rather, it is the transfor-mation of the professional practices of the school that dramatically changed the potential and ability of its students to learn and attain outcomes of signif-icance. The CDSRP recognition was simply a symbol of the transformation.

Does it make a difference to have a vision? According to Grant's team, absolutely, yes!

■ COMMITMENTS: OUR PROMISES THAT WILL MAKE THE VISION COME TRUE

Some cynicism around mission and vision statements is understandable. When all we do is write them, nothing changes. Most organizations, includ-ing schools and districts, have mission statements, and some also have vision statements, but the people in them do not necessarily act in accordance with what they say. It is only when the individuals within an organization begin to *behave* differently that the drive toward the future they have envisioned will commence. A vision can and should inspire, but it is not necessarily an agreement about how to act. The most visionary principal cannot single-handedly cause everyone to start behaving differently. It is shared leadership that creates ownership of a collectively developed mission/purpose and vision. When teachers genuinely share in that development, they will be ready to commit to achieving the mission and making the vision come true. When commitments are made—and written—people are able to hold them-selves and each other accountable to them.

■ PREPARATION FOR THE GC MEETING

This meeting agenda differs from others in this book. The GC meeting you facilitate will simulate a meeting with the full staff, to be co-facilitated by you and GC members. For the Professional Work Plan for this meeting, full staff professional learning will be the best option. This is because revisiting and possibly revising the Mission statement, developing the Vision, and writing Collective Commitments requires all teachers—not just the guiding coalition—to be involved *at the level of development*. But having the GC experience the processes first will enable them to confidently co-facilitate them with you for the staff.

Suggested Meeting Setup:

- Post the Questions of a PLC for reference
- Post the signed Norms poster

Agenda

Guiding Coalition Meeting

1. Review Norms and Assign Meeting Roles

2. Community Building

3. After Action Review

4. Mission, Vision, Commitments

5. Team Planning

6. Tool Kit

7. Evaluate Norms

Writing or Evaluating a Mission Statement

- Does our mission statement define our purpose for existence?
- Does it convey compelling reasons why parents should choose our school, if they had other choices?
- Is it concise?
- Does it describe the ideal for ALL students?
- Is the mission worded in such a way as to hold us accountable, or does it let us off the hook (e.g., dependent on student "potential," for example)?
- Is it durable? Will it still apply several years from now?
- Is the mission worded in such a way that we can immediately define the extent to which we are fulfilling it?
- Does it spur us to action, or does it allow us to remain comfortable with the status quo?

Headlines—Our Vision

Individual Composing (2–3 minutes):

You are in charge of writing the headline for a newspaper that is read throughout the state in an issue three years from now. It is about our school. What does it say?

Collective Commitments

For our vision (headline/s) to come true, what must we all commit to?
Use the blank sentence strips to write "We will..." statements in the following categories:

- Expectations
- Leadership
- Collaboration
- Work of the teacher
- Use of meeting norms and procedures
- Accountability
- Other

Tape each completed statement under the appropriate title on the wall.

Suggested Materials and Equipment for Agenda

- Handouts, three-hole punched
  - Agenda
  - After Action Review
  - Professional Work Plan and Team Commitments for individual note taking, as desired
  - Your school's mission statement, if available
  - Writing or Evaluating a Mission Statement
  - Headlines—Our Vision
  - Collective Commitments
- Sentence strips or 3-inch-wide paper strips, labeled with the following titles, posted high on the walls around the room:
  - Expectations
  - Leadership
  - Collaboration
  - Work of the teacher
  - Use of meetings norms and procedures
  - Accountability
  - Other
- Additional, blank sentence strips or 3-inch-wide paper strips
- Signed Norms poster
- Roles/Responsibilities tent cards
- After Action Review enlarged to poster size
- Chart rack, markers, tape
- Talking Stick
- Poster size copy of agenda posted (or projected)
- Questions of a PLC enlarged to poster size
- Professional Work Plan and Team Commitments enlarged to poster size, including additional copies of page 2 to include all teams
- Parking Lot enlarged to poster size and hung in the meeting area
- Sticky notes, 3x3 inches or larger for potential Parking Lot items
- Tool Kit poster with running list of tools introduced

■ AGENDA NOTES

Mission, Vision, Commitments

Ideally, this GC meeting will serve as a dry run for conducting the processes with the whole staff. If you follow this plan be sure to clarify that for your teacher leaders.

GC members who are willing will then co-facilitate these processes with you at a full-staff professional learning session, which you will plan today during Team Planning.

Mission

I suggest beginning with the school's mission statement, if you have one, and the handout, Writing or Evaluating a Mission Statement. I recommend using the Talking Stick to facilitate a discussion about how well your mission statement aligns to the listed criteria. If you and the teacher leaders are in consensus that it aligns with the criteria, you are ready to move on to Headlines—Our Vision. However, if the GC feels that the mission statement needs revision (or if you need to compose a mission statement for the first time), ask the Recorder to capture suggestions on a blank chart paper.

To focus a *high* level of energy on the task and to avoid dragging out wordsmithing, I suggest asking the Timer to set the clock for 10 minutes. Then ask the Recorder to tear off the finalized mission statement and post it nearby.

Vision

The Headlines—Our Vision handout can be used to have each GC member compose a headline. A read-around works well to share: pass them around the table clockwise to allow everyone to read all other members' headlines. Stop after each member has gotten his or her headline back.

Ask the Recorder to label a new chart Common Elements, and invite an open discussion about what team members noticed about commonalities while the Recorder captures them. (Note: When GC members facilitate this step with the whole staff, the Common Elements can be given to an ad hoc committee, or given back to the GC, for the drafting of a Vision Statement and/or the creation of an illustrated poster.)

Commitments

The Collective Commitments handout was designed for this step. Have the team break into groups of three and join one yourself. Ask each triad to write out "We will . . ." statements for each of the first six categories using the blank sentence strips or paper strips and then tape them under the titles that have been posted around the room. The Other category can be used as needed. When everyone is finished, each title will have a list of strips posted underneath it.

For the next step, break the GC into groups of four to eight members each. Assign each group one of the six (or seven) categories with its taped-up list of "We will . . ." sentence strips.

Give each group a piece of chart paper to write a *succinct*, overall "We will . . ." commitment statement for their assigned category that incorporates the main ideas of all the sentence strips. Groups that finish early can work with another category that has not yet been assigned.

When finished, there will be six to seven "We will . . ." commitment statements written on chart papers. Ask each GC member to sign at the bottom of all the charts.

Remind the team that these processes were for practice. They will co-facilitate the completion of the real documents by the staff as a whole.

Team Planning

The processes described for this GC meeting need to be altered somewhat for the full staff so that each teacher can participate fully and meaningfully. The companion website contains detailed facilitation notes for team planning for Mission, Vision, and Commitments.

Tool Kit

Once the staff has completed them, these become new tools for team leaders to use as ongoing referents for their teams' work: Mission Statement (new or revised), Vision Statement or graphic, and Our Collective Commitments. You may wish to have GC members add them to their individual—and the group's—Tool Kits now.

■ AFTER THE MEETING—PRINCIPAL FOLLOW UP SUGGESTIONS

The full-staff professional learning you have just planned with your GC is an important step. Symbolically, it will represent the transition to shared leadership and to PLC processes. If you did not appoint a Task Reminder as discussed in Chapter 6, include calendar time to personally check and be certain that all preparations are in order before the day of the session, and check in with your GC members to be sure they feel confident and ready to do their parts.

■ SUMMARY

The purpose of this GC meeting is to plan a full-staff professional learning session to clarify, revisit, or create a school mission, vision statement, and develop collective commitments. You will facilitate simulated activities for accomplishing these with the GC, then support the development of a Professional Work Plan for GC members to facilitate them with staff.

 Access links and additional resources at
www.corwin.com/sharedleadership

8

Managing
Complex Change

Why are certain changes so difficult for some people and relatively easy for others? While this is apparent everywhere in life—not just in schools or in job roles—an excellent resource for school leaders for understanding and leading complex change is *School Leadership That Works—From Research to Results* by Robert Marzano, Timothy Waters, and Brian McNulty (2005).

RESEARCH ON EFFECTIVE PRINCIPALS ■

At the conclusion of the meta-analysis that was the foundation for the book, the researchers found that—not surprisingly—principal leadership has a statistically significant impact on student achievement. Twenty-one behaviors emerged from the meta-analysis that described what teachers observed effective principals doing. These behaviors were termed as follows:

Affirmation	Intellectual stimulation
Change agent	Involvement in curriculum, instruction, and assessment
Communication	Knowledge of curriculum, instruction, and assessment
Contingent rewards	Monitor/evaluate

Culture	Optimize
Discipline	Order
Flexibility	Outreach
Focus	Relationships
Ideals/beliefs	Resources
Input	Situational awareness
	Visibility

Unfortunately, some principals react to this list by mistakenly thinking, "Oh, no! Twenty-one more things to do! I have enough initiatives to think about already!" Instead, a more accurate understanding is that these behaviors—each one being a behavior many principals engage in already, at least to some degree—are interpersonal tools that effective principals intentionally employ when leading change initiatives in their schools. A heightened awareness and understanding of them enhances a principal's effectiveness.

The research found that the importance of the individual behaviors varied depending on the kinds of change the principal was leading. The terms *first order change* and *second order change* were coined by the researchers to describe the difference in the kinds of changes principals led in their schools.

First order changes can be described as ordinary, everyday changes that an individual responds to with relative ease, while second order change often presents challenges for the person experiencing it.

A very important related conclusion was that change is highly individual. What is a first order change for one teacher may be a second order change for another. This is why we see some teachers adapting easily to a change, such as a new expectation to collaborate meaningfully with colleagues, while others seem to view it as an anathema.

McREL suggests four categories of reasons (see McREL's graphic, Exhibit 7 on page 88) why a change has either first order or second order implications for an individual. These categories represent the person's perceptions of the change. One category is the individual's belief that they lack sufficient skills and knowledge to implement the change. Sometimes, resistance is a cover-up for fears of having these shortcomings exposed to others. In my experience, this is actually the easiest of the four categories to remedy, through professional development and coaching. More on this shortly.

Another category has to do with an individual's worldview or philosophy regarding the change—what we might think of as his or her personal paradigm. In the case of collaboration, a teacher who holds dear his personal autonomy behind the classroom door, and feels strongly about what was once termed "academic freedom," is likely to have difficulty with the idea of de-privatizing his practice, developing a consistent set of essential learnings for students with his colleagues along with assessments they all will administer, then sharing and analyzing the assessment results publicly (he may, in fact, still be struggling with the very notion of common standards and state/district testing that measures them, which began in most states shortly after No Child Left Behind was enacted in 2001).

Related to this, another category is group norms that do not support the kind of change being implemented. If most members of a grade level or department hold the beliefs just described, the unwritten norms of this group will make the change more difficult for all its members. Other unwritten norms, such as peer pressure to resist administrative leadership, stemming from a historical, adversarial relationship between teachers and administrators, may also contribute to this perception.

Finally, in a fourth category, some teachers will perceive the change as a radical departure from past practice, while others—who experience the change as having only first order implications—see it as a logical next step.

Have you been surprised at some of the teachers on staff who are having difficulty with this particular change? Perhaps you have never known them to be resistant in the past. That is because an individual responds to each change that comes along based on some configuration of these four perceptions. There may be one, two, three, or all four perceptions present. It only takes one of them to make the change second order for the teacher, but any number—including all four—may be present.

What does this mean for you and your teacher leaders as you work with staff members experiencing this change as second order? This is the rub. The second, third, and fourth categories of Perceptions are not easily changed by direct action. How many times in your personal or professional life have you ever succeeded in changing someone's mind through arguing, providing data, rationale, or logic? Very few, probably. However, you—and only you, or another administrator on your administrative team, if you have one—can *require* a staff member to *behave* differently. You can *require* a staff member to attend professional development, work with a coach, prepare for and attend team meetings, and demonstrate professional behavior, and you can provide consequences—respectfully and supportively, of course—if they do not. Then, through having new (increasingly positive) experiences a person changes his or her own mind.

Your teacher leaders, on the other hand, cannot require any colleague to do anything. But they can provide ongoing support to those who are experiencing the change as second order, beginning at the earliest stages, such as when they attend professional development. The team leader can become the teacher's go-to person, who can help the individual be successful in making the transition you are requiring him or her to make. Very important, all the tools you are introducing and practicing each time the GC meets will help the team leader do just that—making team collaborations a safe, respectful, productive experience for every member.

Administrators are important drop-in members of teacher collaborations, too, but since it is impossible to sit in on every collaboration of every team, having your teacher leaders ultra-prepared for this hand-off of leadership is of the utmost importance. Collaborations are their special realm of influence. For the resistors, those for whom collaboration is a second order change, it is through having these new, positive experiences—experiences they are being *required* to have—that they are able to begin to revise their perceptions.

The best news is this: No matter how resistant a teacher may be at the outset, in almost all cases, once he or she has begun to experience true collaboration, he or she is likely to become its most ardent champion. I have seen it so many times it amounts to a Wonder of Shared Leadership.

■ PROFESSIONAL LEARNING: HOW PRINCIPALS WALK THE TALK—OR NOT

I promised to elaborate on the first perception: a teacher's private, perhaps carefully hidden, belief that he or she does not have the skills and knowledge to implement the change. I also said that relative to the other perceptions, it is the easiest to change, through professional development and coaching. Unfortunately, professional learning sessions can range from highly valuable opportunities for educators to gain new skills and knowledge, to incredible wastes of time. Teachers know this—they have been crammed into cafetoriums and multipurpose rooms to be subjected to non-differentiated training that has nothing to do with their own worlds just too many times.

On the flip side, I once spent about a year in an area service agency as a member of various teams that were frequently invited to provide professional learning for schools in just such settings. In my less-than-fond recollections, in too many cases, in spite of our utmost efforts to differentiate the session based on the best information we had about teacher wants and needs, I can relive a too-typical day that is sabotaged from the outset. How? Picture this. In large part, the principal sets the stage. He introduces the team, then promptly disappears—or worse, almost, spends the day in view of his teachers but working on his iPad or talking on his cell phone at the back of the room. The teachers sitting in the top row of the auditorium promptly take out their newspapers (if they ever put them away), and a variety of other audience behaviors begin to emerge to demonstrate clearly to us that the teachers are not a bit more interested in being here than the principal. This is not on the part of all audience members, but enough to make the day less than ideal for those who are genuinely interested, in spite of the energy we expend to monitor and adjust the content and activities on-the-fly in an attempt to optimize a very less-than-optimal situation.

What messages are communicated here by the school leader to the teachers? (1) You need this, but I don't. (2) You will not be held accountable for this, since I have no idea what you are learning. (3) This is not terribly important, and I've got better things to do.

Given a session that is differentiated appropriately for teacher needs and is well planned and executed, please do not misconstrue this to mean that administrators should hulk about the room, policing the session. An effective administrative leader is what Richard and Rebecca DuFour (2012) have termed *the learning leader* (as distinguished from the traditional *instructional leader* of times gone by). I think of one aspect of this role as *the lead learner*. In a case like the one above, a full staff professional learning, the principal—and the assistant principals (APs) if the school has them—intersperse themselves among the teachers, becoming team members for the day. An effective lone ranger principal with no APs is likely to spend one part of the day with one team, move to another after the morning break, and then another after lunch. The purpose is not to monitor the teachers, but to be full participants. For an administrative team, sitting off to the side at an administrators' table simply sends another undesirable message. Lead learner administrators are learning, too, shoulder-to-shoulder with the teachers. They show interest and enthusiasm for the learning. They stay till the end of the day, including any segments set aside for planning next steps to implement the new learning.

When teachers go off site—such as to the district office—for professional learning sessions, is it possible for the principal to attend every one of them? Realistically, probably not. But wise principals are judicious in choosing which sessions to attend. Modeling is everything. The old adage, "Actions speak louder than words," is nowhere truer than in the realm of professional learning.

GUIDING COALITION BOOK STUDIES: USING *SCHOOL LEADERSHIP THAT WORKS* AS A TEAM RESOURCE ■

Many principals find that facilitating professional book studies helps foster new ideas and provides a natural forum for discussing them. I have found that teams of teacher leaders especially benefit from doing book studies with their principals. *School Leadership That Works: From Research to Results* by Marzano et al. (2005) is an excellent team resource. I highly recommend that principals read this book and consider purchasing a copy for each team member. It is not essential to do this before the GC begins to meet; in fact, it may be better to wait until the meetings settle into a routine, because the teacher leaders will have enough on their plates without being handed a book to read! At some point, however, after you have read and digested most of the book, and feel the team is ready, it is a terrific resource. Chapter 7, A Plan for Effective School Leadership, discusses the application of the research in a shared leadership model, with excellent tables summarizing effective teacher leader actions in a shared leadership school, such as Figure 7.4— Leadership Team Actions Supporting the Nine Responsibilities of a Principal. I find all the tables to be very helpful, and my favorite is Figure 7.6—Second-Order Change: Responsibilities That Suffer and Actions That Help. The researchers concluded that during second order change, four of the Responsibilities (Communication, Culture, Input, and Order) require special attention, which the principal alone may not always be able to provide. This table lists specific actions the teacher leaders can take to support those Responsibilities to make the change successful.

ANOTHER RESOURCE: *THE BALANCED LEADERSHIP FRAMEWORK: CONNECTING VISION WITH ACTION* ■

This little gem is available as a free pdf download. Search for *The Balanced Leadership Framework: Connecting Vision With Action* in a search engine. product-54. Authored by former McREL CEO Timothy Waters and Greg Cameron, the booklet summarizes, in a concise, how-to format, the application of the research behind *School Leadership That Works*. I often request that district and site leaders provide this as a team resource for its graphics and easy-to-read summaries. For example, here is a graphic of the four perceptions that make change first or second order for an individual:

Exhibit 7   Comparison of first-order change and second-order change

First-Order	Second-Order
An extension of the past	A break with the past
Within existing paradigms	Outside of existing paradigms
Consistent with prevailing values and norms	Conflicted with prevailing values and norms
Implemented with existing knowledge and skills	Requiring new knowledge and skills to implement

Source: Reprinted by permission of McREL. For additional information on McREL's Balanced Leadership visit www.mcrel.org.

■ A FINAL NOTE ABOUT SECOND-ORDER CHANGE

It is easy to forget that sometimes change can be second order for those leading it, including both principals and teacher leaders. If you selected your GC members based on criteria such as discussed in Chapter 1, it is unlikely that you have encountered outright resistance on your team. But that is not to say that some members may not have doubts, concerns, or fears as the work unfolds—just as you may occasionally experience yourself. Be patient in your team and individual discussions, and do not dismiss these feelings. They are not cause for abandoning the work, but managing complex change requires time and patience. Be patient with yourself and with them.

McREL developed its own theory of change from its research, and identified four phases (Waters & Cameron, 2007). For changes that are first order for most teachers, the phases include creating demand (creating dissatisfaction for the status quo for students, while simultaneously painting a picture of a better future), implementing the change, and monitoring and evaluating the change. The process is cyclical and iterative—steps may need to be repeated as the change unfolds.

However, a fourth step was identified for cases when certain individuals are experiencing the change as second order: managing personal transitions. This is an individualized, personalized step. For this step, the most important of the 21 Leadership Responsibilities is Flexibility, where the leader "adapts his or her leadership behavior to the needs of the current situation, and is comfortable with dissent." As described in the follow up notes for the initial GC Meetings, a leader who effectively fulfills this Responsibility "is directive or non-directive as the situation warrants," and "adapts leadership style to the needs of specific situations." Further, the leader "is comfortable with making major changes in how things are done" (Marzano et al., 2005, p. 49). Are you comfortable with strategically rocking the boat when it is for the betterment of student learning? Are your teacher leaders?

Finally, the leader "encourages people to express diverse opinions contrary to those held by individuals in positions of authority" (Marzano et al., 2005, p. 49). Nowhere is this more important than during your GC meetings, because if these frank discussions cannot happen in that safe place, they cannot happen at all, and this important work will simply grind to a halt.

Take the time to manage personal transitions—for yourself, your team, and for the teachers on your staff.

SUMMARY ■

The concepts of first- and second-order change and the 21 Leadership Responsibilities of effective principals emerged from the research underpinning *School Leadership That Works—From Research to Results* by Robert Marzano et al. (2005). This is an excellent resource for principals developing shared leadership and leading other complex change. Professional learning is important in most complex change, and principals who act as Lead Learners behave in ways that are distinctly different from other principals. They learn shoulder-to-shoulder with their teachers, modeling involvement, and symbolically assigning high importance to the professional learning, while signaling future accountability for implementation.

Access links and additional resources at
www.corwin.com/sharedleadership

9

Discussion Protocols

A Bridge From Meetings-as-Usual to Professional Collaboration

If your team leaders completed the assessment offered in Chapter 6, consider the results. Were most of the results at the high end of the scale (5–6)? If not, a highly effective strategy to move collegial teams toward true collaboration, and to continue to address the needs of teams with some degree of dysfunction, is to begin the use of discussion protocols.

Protocols are formalized ways to hold specific kinds of discussions, resulting in specific kinds of outcomes. Introducing them does not imply that informal, open discussions will no longer be used, but to maximize the valuable and finite resource of team meeting time to accomplish a particular result, their regular use and practice will enable teams to become more efficient and effective. Will protocols always be necessary? Probably not, but even highly functional teams that have worked together for a long period may return to using them from time to time. This can happen when team members have become—as one teacher leader put it—"too comfortable" and less diligent in staying focused until the desired agreement or meeting outcome is achieved. High-level collaboration can sometimes slip back into easy-going—but not very efficient or productive—collegiality.

In many teams that still function at the beginning stages of collaboration ("tea and cookies" collegiality), as well as those that are neither effective nor collegial, meeting behavior follows certain predictable patterns. The unwritten but powerful norms of behavior that have come to be cemented in place prohibit a departure from these patterns. A protocol serves to break that pattern, much like the scripts a therapist may introduce to couples and families who have problems communicating and cannot seem to break old, predictable patterns of interaction.

Consider Robert's Rules of Order. Imagine a meeting where they are typically used—a city council, school board, PTA, or the meeting of any legislative body—without them. Quite possibly, some individuals resisted them when they were first introduced in the late nineteenth century, preferring free discussions instead. But while highly artificial, they keep meetings on track and reduce wasted time. Similarly, discussion protocols are simply a structure for educators to accomplish significantly more and better work in a strictly limited amount of time.

After GC members feel a degree of comfort with protocols, to begin implementation with teams, you will need to communicate an explicit expectation to the staff to do so. Protocols are unnatural. Team members may resist the artificiality and initial discomfort of using them. "We just want to have an open discussion!" is a common objection. In the beginning, team members may even mockingly use the language of the protocol to express their resistance. But if team leaders can persist through the initial stages of using protocols, the benefits will quickly become apparent.

■ THE MANY VARIETIES OF PROTOCOLS

Many teams welcome the use of protocols, immediately seeing and experiencing their value. These teams quickly move to writing their own protocols, which can be considered an important milestone in team development. Googling "discussion protocols" will yield a rich source for using both as-is and modifying.

The next chapter outlines a guiding coalition (GC) meeting to introduce protocols. When considering protocols, the Student Work Protocol is a good place to begin, because all teams can use it. Course-alike teams, vertical teams, and teams of specialists can all benefit from using this discussion tool.

Elementary principals of schools large enough to have grade-level teams of at least three to four members may wish to skip the Student Work Protocol and go directly to Chapter 11, which introduces the Student-Based Protocol—designed for teams where all the teachers teach the same subject and/or content and can thus use and develop common assessments/ assignments. However, the Student Work Protocol still has benefits for course-alike teams, so be sure to take a look at Chapter 10 before deciding.

Chapter 12 introduces a planning/problem-solving protocol adapted from Mike Schmoker's (1999a) 30 Minute Meeting, outlined in *Results: The Key to Continuous School Improvement*. Once your teacher leaders have experienced the protocols introduced in these chapters and tried them a couple of times with their teams, they will be ready to write their own protocols for a variety of purposes and/or modify those they have learned.

If you have the luxury of convening your GC for a full day, I recommend combining these three GC meetings into one session. But whether you work with these protocols in separate meetings or one meeting, I urge you to continue to incorporate the best practice agenda items introduced thus far, along with the new protocol item(s) so that they become routine for your teacher leaders. Your modeling of their use, each time the GC meets, signals their importance and value.

TRY IT, THEN CHANGE IT ■

In my experience, it is best to ask team leaders to try out each protocol at least twice with their teams, with no modifications. This is because of the inherent temptation to give in to the pressure of team member resistance (e.g., Let's just try it without the timer!). These kinds of suggestions at the beginning stages will usually serve to defeat the very purpose of using a protocol (akin to accepting Robert's Rules of Order as long as, for example, motions are not used). Each protocol presented here has been fire-tested and refined with many teams at all levels. When a team says, "This is just weird. We like our open discussions better," I counter with my standard response that I mentioned in Chapter 4—"Just try it. Let it be weird. It's OK." Typically, that team will not only embrace the protocol, but also will confide to me by the end of the series, "You know, we write our own protocols now."

THE IMPORTANCE OF THE TIMER ■

A key feature of each protocol is Timekeeper role. Remember that protocols are a bridge from meetings-as-usual to highly effective collaboration. A common complaint about meetings-as-usual is that they accomplish so little. Having a timed agenda is an immediate game changer. It is also the first feature of protocols that teachers are most eager to discard. No matter how a team eventually modifies a discussion protocol, it can virtually always be successful to accomplish the desired result as long as the agenda items are timed. As stated before, this is not to say that any given team will always need protocols, but once the team stops using a timer, the team leader should be clear on his or her intention, and the team's readiness to do so, because they are definitely moving from the realm of protocols back into open discussions.

INTRODUCING THE CONCEPT ■
OF DISCUSSION PROTOCOLS

The following tools are presented here instead of within the following GC Meetings because you may, for example, elect to introduce protocols with the Student Work Protocol, perhaps skipping the others. Regardless, consider using some of or all the following documents as handouts to introduce protocols to your teacher leaders. Included with the handouts is an individual survey—Does My Team Need Protocols?—which may be helpful for GC members to complete.

What Is a Protocol?

Definition: An "unnatural conversation," designed to maximize the use of meeting time and minimize wasted time, for the purpose of accelerating improved student learning in all team members' classrooms.

Common Features:

- Set time frames for each discussion step
- Roles
- Facilitator—diligently keeps group on track
- Timekeeper—diligently reminds group when it's time to move on
- Parking Lot for items not germane to the discussion at hand
- Record keeping: group memory (charting) or individual forms, or both
- Use of norms (developed, posted, reviewed, monitored/reminded, evaluated)

What Are Protocols For?

Protocols are a BRIDGE from traditional department and grade-level meetings to highly effective collaboration.

Common Uses of Protocols:

- Analyzing student work samples and assessment results to improve instructional practices and catch students before they fail
- Analyzing large-scale assessments (e.g., quarterly benchmarks) to conduct an "autopsy" on the curriculum and instruction that was used and plan for future improvements
- Evaluating effective use of newly adopted materials
- Evaluating use of specific instructional strategies and their impact on students
- Setting and evaluating SMARTe Goals
- Problem solving ("What can we do about the homework problem?")
- Planning

Should a protocol be used every time the team meets? Probably not, but if the team is marginally effective, new to collaboration, or has dysfunctional interactions or member behaviors, they should be used most of the time until collaboration improves.

Can new protocols be written by teachers/teams? YES!

Protocols

Traditional Department & Grade-Level Meetings

Advanced Collaboration

Protocols are the BRIDGE

Why Protocols?

"Protocols are weird. We'd rather just have an open discussion."

A Leadership Team Member

Alexander Platt and colleagues (2008) defined five levels of team functioning. Level 5, Accountable Teams, may typically work without protocols.

Protocols are *very* useful when collaboration is new.

Protocols disrupt overly comfortable—or dysfunctional—patterns of group discourse to enhance productivity.

Does My Team Need Protocols?

1. Our team meetings rarely get off topic and complaining is rare.

   True   False

   1   2   3   4   5

2. Meetings are always productive—we do not waste peoples' time.

   True   False

   1   2   3   4   5

3. I consistently leave the meeting with new strategies for my most challenging students.

   True   False

   1   2   3   4   5

4. Our team grades have improved dramatically since we began collaborating.

   True   False   Don't Know

   1   2   3   4   5   6

5. Our team scores on common assessments, including informal assessments (e.g., weekly/biweekly), quarterly benchmarks, and so on have improved dramatically since we began collaborating.

   True   False   Don't Know

   1   2   3   4   5   6

6. Students in our team cannot fall through the cracks. We have team interventions built into our schedule for students who need a re-teaching loop, while others get enrichment/extension.

   True   False

   1   2   3   4   5

7. We assist each other with strategies for students who have behavior, family, and motivation issues.

   True   False

   1   2   3   4   5

8. Members of this team rely on each other, and team members would say that collaboration reduces their workload. We share the work of developing common assessments and lesson designs for the whole team.

   True   False

   1   2   3   4   5

Use Protocols If . . .

Team meetings

- tend to wander off topic,
- often do not finish all business in the time allocated,
- often leave members feeling little or nothing was accomplished,
- have a tendency toward too much socializing,
- are impacted by a negative history between some members, or
- are impacted by dysfunctional behaviors (hostility, lack of respect, etc.).

Purpose of Protocols:
To improve student learning
through continuously adjusting
our classroom practice

Venn Diagram Comparing Student Work Protocol and Student-Based Protocol

You may wish to use the following Venn Diagram with GC members if you introduce both the Student Work Protocol and the Student-Based Protocol. This can be enlarged to poster size and used as a basis for a discussion to compare the two protocols after the team has tried them both.

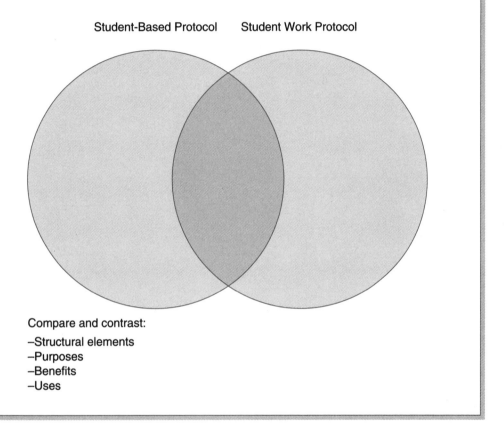

Student-Based Protocol   Student Work Protocol

Compare and contrast:

–Structural elements
–Purposes
–Benefits
–Uses

■ **SUMMARY**

Protocols are somewhat analogous to Robert's Rules of Order. They provide a predictable structure that disrupts normal patterns of interaction, making every minute count in team collaborations, and keeping discussions on track. Resistance is not uncommon when protocols are introduced, but their value and versatility make them one of the most powerful tools for teacher leaders to help their teams improve student outcomes.

Access links and additional resources at
www.corwin.com/sharedleadership

10

Guiding Coalition Meeting

Student Work Protocol

This protocol is so named because it moves teacher discussions from numeric test or quiz data to the examination of physical examples of student work. Some versions are called *tuning protocols*, because their intent is to help professionals fine-tune their practice.

A major advantage of this discussion tool is that no matter how different the subject matter or grade levels represented among the team members may be, the teachers' professional expertise as instructors will enable them to make valuable suggestions to the presenting teacher. Most important, everyone benefits from the sharing of suggestions, most of which will turn out to be applicable in some way to everyone's areas of instruction. In vertical teams, this sharing contributes to improved articulation; in diverse teams such as teams of specialists, it often sparks ideas for other kinds of professional collaboration. Course-alike teams who regularly discuss common assessments also benefit from occasionally using this protocol for a deeper look at instructional practice in a particular kind of lesson.

In this protocol, one teacher on the team will bring a set of copies of student work for each of the other members. I recommend that the presenting teacher select six students whose work will be shared:

- two students typical of those who attained the objective of the lesson
- two students typical of those who almost—but not quite—attained the objective
- two students typical of those who missed the boat

If collaboration is new, presenting teachers may wish to white out the student names. Over time, the development of the view that "all students are everyone's students" will eliminate this need.

The presenting teacher also brings copies of an outline of the lesson/instructional activity, including the expected learning (objective) that the students were to demonstrate by the end of the lesson, with criteria for mastery/attainment. It is also helpful to bring any student handouts or other aids that were used so that the team can grasp all the instructional strategies and supports that went into the lesson.

Finally, the presenting teacher crafts a focusing question for the team to consider. This may be something like, "Although everyone attained the objective, I'm looking for ideas for increasing the Depth of Knowledge in the rest of this unit," or "My students learning English struggled with this. I would like ideas for reteaching as well as scaffolding future lessons like this."

A crucial point for teams to understand when beginning this protocol is that taking one's turn as presenting teacher does not imply, "I need help—please help me." Teams of highly expert teachers benefit from discussing next steps with colleagues and having collaborative discussions about moving their practice to the next level.

■ PREPARATION FOR PRESENTING THE PROTOCOL

I have found that simply going over the steps of the protocol is not sufficient for teacher leaders to feel comfortable returning to their teams to try it out. Instead, I now typically do two things. First, I show video clips of the protocol in use (see Facilitation Notes for Agenda Item #4 for YouTube links), stopping after each step for group discussion. Then, we simulate the protocol as a team. Over the years I have collected student work samples from various levels for this purpose, along with the lesson outlines and focusing questions. Before the videos were created, I simply conducted the simulation. I recommend at least doing the simulation with the guiding coalition (GC) so that the teacher leaders can experience it before attempting to lead it.

To do this, you will need to act as either the protocol facilitator or the presenting teacher. If you are going to role play the presenting teacher, you will need to work with a teacher on staff—this may or may not be a teacher who is a GC member—to obtain student work samples as described above and the lesson outline. Then you will need to craft a focusing question for the group to consider. I recommend working ahead of time with another GC member (ideally, not the one who contributed the work, if it was a team member) who will serve as the protocol facilitator. It will be helpful for that person to preview the video clips of the protocol, whether the clips are used in the GC meeting or not.

The other option for a simulation is to ask a GC member with whom you have a high level of mutual trust if he or she would be willing to serve as the presenting teacher, using student work samples and providing the other materials described above, based on a recent lesson, and you will be the protocol facilitator. This obviously requires some degree of courage on the teacher's part. My preference is usually to role-play the presenting teacher myself. When I work with a cohort of teams, I generally work ahead of time with the principals, who serve as presenting teachers using my work samples and other materials, and have each of them select a team member to serve as the protocol facilitator after we have viewed and discussed the video clips as a full group.

One important note, during Group Discussion, it makes a huge difference for the presenting teacher to physically pull away from the table and take his or her own notes on an electronic or paper tablet and for group members to refer to the teacher *in the third person*. This prevents the presenting teacher from joining the discussion prematurely. The opportunity to respond to whatever suggestions and affirmations the teacher chooses will be in the next step, when the teacher can pull his or her chair back up to the table and symbolically rejoin the group, and at which time he or she will solely have the floor.

Suggested Meeting Setup:

- Post the Questions of a PLC for reference
- Post the signed Norms poster

Agenda

Guiding Coalition Meeting

1. Review Norms and Assign Meeting Roles

2. Community Building

3. After Action Review

4. Student Work Protocol

5. Team Planning

6. Tool Kit

7. Evaluate Norms

Student Work Protocol With Facilitator's Notes

Approximate Time Frame: 35 minutes

Introduction	• Introduce presenting teacher • Review norms • Get volunteer to be in charge of Parking Lot • Review protocol steps	1–2 minutes
Presenting Teacher	• Invite presenting teacher to share the lesson, objective, strategies used, student work samples, and focusing question.	5 minutes
Review the Focusing Question	• Reread the focusing question for the group.	
Clarifying Questions	• Invite clarifying questions. • Remind group not to start giving feedback—questions should be clarifying only. "Have you thought about …?" is feedback disguised as a clarifying question.	5 minutes
Silent Idea Generating	• Ask team members to write suggestions **as well as positive feedback** (facilitator also writes feedback). • One idea per sticky note • If needed, remind members this is silent writing time.	5 minutes
Group Discussion	• Presenting teacher pulls away from the table and uses a tablet for note taking. • Invite team members to share ideas they wrote, including both positive feedback and suggestions. • Remind group not to speak directly to presenting teacher; use third person when referring to the person, as if he or she was not present.	10 minutes
Presenting Teacher Response	• Invite presenting teacher to respond to any parts of the feedback that he or she CHOOSES to—remind group that this is only the presenting teacher talking.	5 minutes
Collect All Ideas	• Pass all sticky notes to presenting teacher.	
Debriefing	• Discuss protocol itself (presenting teacher has now returned to the table and joins the general discussion). • How the process went • Whether time frames were adequate for each step • To what degree norms were followed	2 minutes
Parking Lot	• As time allows, discuss any Parking Lot items. OR, if none, • Thank the presenter and group. • Review date of next team meeting and who is presenting and facilitating.	

This is an adaptation of a protocol developed by the Riverside County Office of Education. Reprinted with permission from the Riverside County Office of Education. For more information on educational support and services, please visit www.rcoe.us.

Suggested Materials and Equipment for Agenda

- Handouts, three-hole punched

  - Agenda
  - After Action Review
  - Any handouts from Chapter 9 that you feel may be useful as a general introduction to protocols
  - Student Work Protocol
  - Copies of the presenting teacher's work samples for each team member
  - Copies of the presenting teacher's lesson outline for each team member
  - Copies of the presenting teacher's Focusing Question for each team member
  - Copies for team members of any additional materials the presenting teacher used in the lesson with students
  - Professional Work Plan and Team Commitments for individual note taking, as desired

- 3x3-inch sticky notes for writing feedback
- Electronic or paper tablet with rigid backing for presenting teacher to take notes during Group Discussion
- Video projection system if video clips will be used
- Signed Norms poster
- Roles/Responsibilities tent cards
- After Action Review enlarged to poster size
- Chart rack, markers, tape
- Talking Stick
- Questions of a PLC enlarged to poster size
- Professional Work Plan and Team Commitments enlarged to poster size, including additional copies of page 2 to include all teams
- Parking Lot enlarged to poster size and hung in the meeting area
- Sticky notes, 3x3 inches or larger for potential Parking Lot items
- Tool Kit poster with running list of tools introduced

■ AGENDA NOTES

Student Work Protocol

If this is the GC's first experience with protocols, I suggest using some of the handouts from Chapter 9 as a general introduction.

As you simulate this protocol with the GC, it is helpful for the Timer to nonverbally signal a 1-minute warning when timing each protocol step.

If you decide to introduce the protocol using one of the suggested videos, invite team members to take notes during each segment. Then stop the video and discuss each step before playing the next segment. The Focusing Question segment may be combined with the step before or after; all the steps were edited during post-production so that they are shorter than the time segments indicated in the protocol outline. I strongly advise against showing the entire video at once. Participants gain much more from viewing and discussing each segment. You may also skip all the introductory material and go directly to the first protocol step.

Go to the YouTube site and search for *Tuning Protocol: Fine Tuning Our Classroom Practice with Presenting Teacher Donn Cushing* and *Tuning Protocol: Fine Tuning Our Classroom Practice with Presenting Teacher Gareth Richards*.

While both these videos were produced with a high school team of specialists, they are good examples of how a team at any level can engage in high level collaboration based on student work.

If you are unable to load these particular videos for some reason, many other good examples of similar protocols are available on YouTube and TeacherTube, best found by searching for Tuning Protocol.

Tool Kit

The Student Work Protocol can be added to GC members' individual Tool Kits and the team's Tool Kit.

AFTER THE MEETING—PRINCIPAL FOLLOW UP SUGGESTIONS ■

As you reflect on this meeting, consider the ease or difficulty with which each team leader met the challenge of trying out protocols. If a team leader has difficulty or is clearly uncomfortable with protocols, the likelihood of his or her team having success with them is small. If the GC has decided to move ahead with protocols, these are the teams you will want to prioritize for drop-in visits during collaboration. Be prepared to balance your leadership; you never want to usurp a GC member's leadership when he or she is facilitating a team meeting. In fact, if the team leader tries to hand off leadership to you, do not be tempted to step into the role. Simply defer to the leader by saying something like, "I'm here to support this team in any way I can, and I have confidence in you all and your leader to try this out to move your collaboration to the next level." But if you are asked a specific question, or if there is a natural opening where you can offer encouragement, clarification, restate expectations, or help the team with a step or section of a protocol that simply does not seem to be working, that is appropriate and supportive.

Also, remember that you never have to be in the position of having all the answers. That is why you are developing shared leadership. So you can also say something like, "We are still figuring this out together. My advice is to try this out, make notes about what works and doesn't work when you come to the Debrief step, and the guiding coalition will revisit this next time we meet."

TROUBLESHOOTING ■

At each point in the journey where a new expectation is introduced, there will be a new level of teacher concern, perhaps along with pressure from staff to stop the progress of the work, or better yet to some minds, abandon it completely and return to the status quo of the good ol' days of before it all began. "Stop! This is moving too fast! We have enough on our plates! It's [parent conference time, end of the grading period, approaching the holiday season, etc. etc.]." Your teacher leaders will be feeling the brunt of this, although your more veteran staff may come directly to you with these objections as well.

Sadly, I have seen the most promising beginnings come to a screeching halt when principals are personally unable to resist this pressure and/or do not know how to support their teacher leaders who face it constantly with peers.

If you are truly committed to the work, your own courage in the face of this pressure will be absolutely essential. Your whole staff—but your teacher leaders in particular—are watching for this. "She caved," one teacher leader told me sadly about her principal, "and everything has stopped." I described this case in Chapter 2; it only took two veteran teachers—first one, then the next—coming in to complain to the principal for her to recant her expectations for the next steps her leadership team had spent 2 days carefully planning. Needless to say, she was never able to regain the trust of these teacher leaders, and the school immediately reverted to its tradition of teacher independence and isolation, with struggling students blamed for their own failure to succeed.

What if you are worried that everything might really be moving too fast or that the teachers' cries about overload have at least some legitimacy? First, here are several things *not* to do: For one, do not convene gripe sessions, under the heading of "focus group" or some other title. This does absolutely nothing but undermine your GC teachers and all the work you have done together. Handle individual teachers' complaints and concerns in a *private*, respectful manner. If a teacher challenges you publicly, acknowledge his or her concern and then invite the teacher to meet with you afterward privately. If some meeting—such as a staff meeting—is already scheduled and you and your teacher leaders are aware of ominous rumblings, be sure to have a Parking Lot posted so that gripes as well as legitimate concerns can be acknowledged and collected to be addressed outside the group setting. Having a prepublished and posted agenda of the planned business of the meeting will help prevent it from becoming derailed into a gripe session. If you should decide to allocate any time on the agenda to concerns (which, please understand, will result in complaints and pressure to put the brakes on, and I do *not* recommend it), be certain to allot a specific, *limited* number of minutes to the item, with ground rules (use your Norms) about how long any individual can take the floor, with a Timer providing a 10-second warning when the speaker's time is almost up. Stop the speaker when time is up if he or she does not honor the Timer's signal. Do not make any public commitments to stop the work, or to change any of the decisions you have made in shared leadership with your teacher leaders, and do not imply that any kind of action will be taken to abandon or slow down implementation. Simply listen and assure complainers that you will consider their concerns. Never allow yourself to be pressured into taking a vote. If a teacher calls for a vote, calmly respond with something like, "This is not up for a vote. We have your concerns captured on the Parking Lot, and we will discuss them the next time the guiding coalition meets. [Joe], you are welcome to drop in anytime tomorrow afternoon and discuss this with me in person."

All this said, I never recommend handling this kind of pressure in a group setting, but sometimes a principal can find himself or herself trapped in an unexpected situation where this emerges. If you find that the situation has become this contentious, I recommend reflecting on how well you are managing the personal transitions for the teachers who are so strongly resisting the change. Have you worked with them privately on a one-to-one basis, balancing your leadership with them by listening, then responding by stepping up and clarifying expectations, and stepping back to offer support? Managing personal transitions is a time-intensive endeavor, and it is absolutely essential for you to invest the time so that the teachers can be successful with the change.

See Chapter 16 for more suggestions on working with challenging individuals.

Now, what *to* do, proactively, as you hear teachers' pleas for relief from the new expectations? As you continue to meet with the guiding coalition, consider whether a *short* and *temporary* hiatus will really help, such as waiting until the week of parent conferences are over to introduce a new discussion protocol. This should be a serious GC discussion, never a unilateral decision and decree from the principal's office. This discussion is a good time to use the talking stick—be sure all voices are heard as you establish consensus on the decision. You want to have the group weigh all the pros and cons to ensure that it doesn't feel like a permanent setback to any of the teacher leaders. Be sure to agree on a definite *endpoint* for any such time-out from the work that you will establish with the staff. Without this, it is very easy for all progress to simply fade away. This clearly communicates that you have listened, heard, and responded to concerns, but that the work is not going to be abandoned. Never acquiesce to backtracking or undoing any of the routines, procedures, and development efforts—such as work on common assignments and assessments—that team leaders have finally begun to get into place with their teams. Promote these gains at every opportunity—in bulletins, e-mail, and in group settings. And if you and your guiding coalition decide on any temporary time-out, once the brief hiatus is over, it's over, and the work moves forward.

Your ability to balance your leadership will continue to be essential as you support your teacher leaders, and all your teachers, in managing personal transitions—stepping up and restating or clarifying expectations, and stepping back to coach, question, and guide. Keep reminding everyone of your purpose: the reason you have embarked on the journey of shared leadership to develop your school as a professional learning community is to ensure the success of all students. *Kids Can't Wait* has been the title of numerous education initiatives. They can't. There is no time to waste.

■ SUMMARY

The Student Work Protocol is a good introductory protocol, because it can be used by vertical teams, diverse teams such as teams of specialists, and course-alike teams. Using this agenda, you will plan a simulation of the SWP for the guiding coalition, enabling them, in turn, to introduce it to their own teams.

Access links and additional resources at
www.corwin.com/sharedleadership

11

Guiding Coalition Meeting

Student-Based Protocol

While crafting this protocol, I was working with cohorts of teams from high performing schools and individual schools in state sanctions. One corrective action that sanctioned schools had to complete was implementing a "student achievement monitoring system [with] use of data to monitor student progress on curriculum-embedded assessments and modify instruction." While poring over tomes of annual state-test-results printouts was not unfamiliar then, especially for the sanctioned schools—some, quite frankly, had been practically beaten to death with it—a workable method for looking, student-by-student, at progress throughout the year was desperately needed. Using various ideas I found online and elsewhere, I distilled them into this protocol, which has since been used by countless course-alike teams from a full range of schools at all levels. As the name implies, the student-based protocol moves the discussion from data on groups—as in analyzing state test data—to individual students.

This protocol is for teams of teachers who all teach the same course—an elementary grade level whose members all teach the same subjects, or the teachers of one secondary subject course. It is for analyzing the results of common assignments, common short-cycle quizzes or performance assessments—in short, anything that the team devises or agrees to use in common to assess student progress and plan upcoming instruction. I will use the term *common assessments* to include all these.

It works best for the common assessment to be focused on a very specific set of skills and competencies, or else to select a subset of the assessment for purposes of discussion. The high school Algebra I team featured in the video link I share was using their weekly quiz as the focus of their collaboration when they first tried this protocol. They found that the quiz covered too many concepts to be adequately addressed during their weekly collaboration time. They quickly decided to limit the quiz to three items, all on one concept, but with progressive levels of difficulty. Obviously, they did not stop *teaching* all their other content. They simply began to intentionally choose what they felt were the most essential, enduring, high-leverage concepts to be worthy of assessing and then devoting their limited collaboration time to discussing.

The elementary school video I reference in this chapter features the first team to ever try this protocol. Their school was in sanctions, and this team was one of the most open and willing to embrace the use of this new kind of tool. The weakness of the protocol when I first created it was that it did not include a preview of upcoming instruction, which was remedied by the time the Algebra I team used it. So if you choose to use the elementary video, be aware of that issue.

■ PREPARATION FOR PRESENTING THE PROTOCOL

As discussed in the previous chapter, simply handing out the protocol steps and going over them does not give teacher leaders the confidence they need to lead it with peers. As with the Student Work Protocol, I recommend at least simulating the protocol as a guiding coalition, and if time permits, preface that with viewing a video of the protocol in use, stopping to discuss each step before showing the clip of the next one.

For this simulation, you can act as the Facilitator, with the GC members role-playing being members of a specific, course-alike team. Working with either a teacher on the GC or another teacher with whom you have high mutual trust—and in either case, for purposes of the simulation, the teacher's identity can be confidential, with student names whited out—you will again need to obtain copies of student work from a specific assignment or quiz, already graded. Each GC member will be given *different students' work to present and discuss*, as if they were presenting work from their own classes. You will also have a set of student work to share and discuss, just as you would as the teacher leader of a course-alike team. You could also use brief video clips of individual student performances, which works well for PE and performing arts classes. Whole class sets are not necessary; a small sampling of work ranging from high to low student success is all that each member needs. As with the Student Work Protocol, including two samples each for successful, almost successful (review), and students who completely missed the objective (reteach) is a good rule of thumb for collaboration. For simulation purposes, only one of each is sufficient. Duplicate copies are not needed. The Algebra I team in the secondary video uses a document camera to project examples of work being discussed. This is ideal but not absolutely necessary, as you will see if you view the elementary video.

Suggested Meeting Setup:

- Post the Questions of a PLC for reference
- Post the signed Norms poster

Agenda

Guiding Coalition Meeting

1. Review Norms and Assign Meeting Roles

2. Community Building

3. After Action Review

4. Student-Based Protocol

5. Team Planning

6. Tool Kit

7. Evaluate Norms

Student-Based Protocol With Facilitator's Notes

Approximate Time Frame: 45 minutes

Introduction	• Convene group and set purpose (which assignment, quiz, etc. will be discussed) • Ensure that members have brought their target students' work • Review norms • Review protocol steps	1–2 minutes
Successes	• Using ordered sharing, have each team member share what strategy/ies from the last meeting worked well, and how many students in the teacher's target section attained the objective (Recorder records strategies and numbers)	5 minutes
Challenges	• Either project student work or have individual members share features of typical "review" and "reteach" student work. Discuss errors made and what skills or concepts need to be reviewed/retaught for the students in each of these categories (Recorder records these). Continue until all common errors are presented or until time is up.	10 minutes
Team Brainstorm	• Facilitate brainstorming of strategies for reviewing and reteaching. • Recorder charts all ideas. • During discussion, each team member records his or her own notes about how he or she plans to address the review/reteach students. • Recorder should capture any tangent ideas or concerns on the Parking Lot.	10 minutes
Upcoming Instruction	• Facilitate open discussion of concepts or skills that the team will next assess for collaboration. • Ask for ideas for frontloading/scaffolding for students likely to have difficulty, as well as general instructional strategies. • Recorder charts all ideas, including Parking Lot as needed.	15 minutes
Selection	• Team members record their own plans for frontloading/scaffolding, as well as general instructional strategies. • Use ordered sharing for each team member to describe individual plans with the group.	2 minutes

Debriefing	<ul><li>Discuss protocol itself</li><li>How the process went</li><li>Whether time frames were adequate for each step</li><li>To what degree norms were followed</li></ul>	2 minutes
Parking Lot	<ul><li>As time allows, discuss any Parking Lot items OR, if none,</li><li>Thank the group</li><li>Review date of next team meeting and summarize what to bring</li></ul>	

This is an adaptation of a protocol developed by the Riverside County Office of Education. Reprinted with permission from the Riverside County Office of Education. For more information on educational support and services, please visit www.rcoe.us·

Suggested Materials and Equipment for Agenda

- Handouts, three-hole punched

  o Agenda
  o After Action Review
  o Handouts you may have chosen from Chapter 9 if this is the GC's first experience with protocols
  o Student Work Protocol
  o Copies of different sets of student work for each team member and the facilitator; each set including a sample from a student who met the objective, one who almost (but not quite) met the objective, and a student who missed the boat
  o Professional Work Plan and Team Commitments for individual note taking, as desired

- Document camera, if available
- Video projection system if video clips will be used
- Signed Norms poster
- Roles/Responsibilities tent cards
- After Action Review enlarged to poster size
- Chart rack, markers, tape
- Talking Stick
- Poster size copy of agenda posted (or projected)
- Questions of a PLC enlarged to poster size
- Professional Work Plan and Team Commitments enlarged to poster size, including additional copies of page 2 to include all teams
- Parking Lot enlarged to poster size and hung in the meeting area
- Sticky notes, 3x3 inches or larger for potential Parking Lot items
- Tool Kit poster with running list of tools introduced

■ AGENDA NOTES

Student-Based Protocol

If the Student-Based Protocol is the first protocol you are bringing to the GC, consider choosing from the handouts in Chapter 9 as a general introduction to protocols. When simulating this protocol, it is helpful for the Timer to nonverbally signal a 1-minute warning when timing each protocol step. Although the secondary video features the Facilitator also serving as Recorder, it is simpler for these roles to be separate when the protocol is new to the team.

If you decide to introduce the protocol using one of the videos, invite team members to take notes during each segment. Then stop to discuss each step before playing the next segment. The 2-minute steps may be combined with the steps before or after. All the steps were edited during post-production so that they are shorter than the time segments indicated in the protocol outline. I strongly advise against showing the entire video at once. Participants gain much more from viewing and discussing each segment. You may also skip all the introductory material and go directly to the first protocol step.

From the YouTube site, search for *Student-Based Protocol and Elementary Math Data Protocol* both by RCOE TV.

The first video, *Student-Based Protocol*, featuring the Moreno Valley High School Algebra I team, includes an additional step for math coach input. The second video, *Elementary Math Data Protocol*, features the fourth-grade teachers at Nan Sanders Elementary using an early version of the protocol to discuss a math assessment. If you use the second video, please note that it does not include the important protocol step for previewing specific skills in upcoming instruction.

If you are unable to load these particular videos for some reason, many other good examples of similar protocols are available on YouTube and TeacherTube.

Tool Kit

The Student-Based Protocol can be added to GC members' individual Tool Kits and the team's Tool Kit.

AFTER THE MEETING—PRINCIPAL FOLLOW UP SUGGESTIONS ■

Please refer to the Principal Follow Up Suggestions and Troubleshooting notes at the end of Chapter 10.

SUMMARY ■

The Student-Based Protocol (SBP) employs both data and student work samples and is designed for course-alike teams. Teachers will analyze student learning from a highly targeted, brief, short-term assessment, identify gaps in learning and plan for improved instruction, and preview upcoming instruction. Using this agenda, you will plan a simulation of the SBP for the guiding coalition, enabling them, in turn, to introduce it to their own teams.

Access links and additional resources at
www.corwin.com/sharedleadership

12

Guiding
Coalition Meeting

Planning/Problem Solving Protocol

This highly versatile protocol is an adaptation of Mike Schmoker's 30 Minute Meeting. It can be used for problem solving and/or planning. It is a high-energy protocol, with part of the discussion—brainstorming—conducted with the team standing up; an important feature of that step focuses an intense level of creativity on the topic or issue. I was surprised at what a difference this made when I participated in one of Dr. Schmoker's (1999b) workshops. The adaptation presented here requires approximately 40 minutes. Because it does not introduce an expectation of having teachers share personal student work or data, this protocol is sometimes a good beginning choice for moving toward using protocols in teams, because it does not typically generate new levels of anxiety or push-back.

PREPARATION FOR ■
PRESENTING THE PROTOCOL

This protocol is very easy to simulate, and in fact, it is a protocol the GC may find very useful for its own authentic business of planning and problem solving. This chapter includes a set of 7 chart headers, based on Schmoker's *Results* meetings and his brainstorming guidelines.

I recommend downloading these from the online resources, enlarging them to full page size on a copier, cutting them apart, then taping each one to the top of a piece of chart paper in a flip pad on a chart rack so that as facilitator, as you finish one step, you simply flip to the next chart. Using the pre-printed chart headers saves the time of writing the headings by hand each time you flip to a new page. Each chart header in the downloadable file includes, in small print, the number of the step in the sequence of the protocol and the number of minutes allocated to that step. The New Ideas (brainstorming) chart header also includes a brief list of reminders.

You will note that in contrast to the Student Work Protocol and Student-Based Protocol, the time frame for Successes is longer than Challenges. That is because this kind of discussion needs to focus on past successes and avoid bogging down in tangential problems that may not contribute to a solution or viable plan.

Suggested Meeting Setup:

- Post the Questions of a PLC for reference
- Post the signed Norms poster

Agenda

Guiding Coalition Meeting

1. Review Norms and Assign Meeting Roles

2. Community Building

3. After Action Review

4. Planning/Problem Solving Protocol

5. Team Planning

6. Tool Kit

7. Evaluate Norms

Chart Headers

FOCUSING QUESTION

SUCCESSES

What has worked to help us with _____ (focusing question topic) or something similar in the past?

CHALLENGES

Our chief challenges/barriers to _____ (focusing question). (3 minutes)

BRAINSTORMING

NEW IDEAS ABOUT _____ (focusing question)

ACTION PLAN

What   By (when)   Who
_____

EVIDENCE THAT OUR PLAN/STRATEGIES ARE WORKING

PARKING LOT

Adapted from Schmoker, M. (1999). *Results: The Key to Continuous School Improvement.* Workshop booklet, Riverside, CA.

Planning/Problem Solving
Protocol With Facilitator's Notes

Approximate Time Frame: 40 minutes

Focusing Question	• With the team, craft a Focusing Question for the issue or planning topic to be addressed. • On the chart with the Focusing Question chart header, print the question in very large text so that it fills the page. • Tear off this page and post it on the wall next to the chart stand. Be sure everyone can see the posted Focusing Question.	5 minutes
Successes	• Flip to Successes page. • Referring to the topic or issue, facilitate a discussion of past successes—what has helped this team in the past when confronted with a planning topic or issue to be resolved?	5 minutes
Challenges	• Flip to Challenges page. • Referring to the topic or issue, facilitate a discussion of current barriers—what challenges or parameters should the team be aware of, as it works on this planning topic or issue to be resolved?	3 minutes
New Ideas—Team Brainstorm	• Flip to New Ideas page • This is the heart of the protocol. Ask team members to **stand up, gather around the chart, and stand in a half circle.** • Use ordered sharing. • Each team member will contribute one idea per round, speaking for up to 20 seconds. • Ask the Timer to keep strict time, with a nonverbal signal. • Recorder will chart words and phrases—not complete sentences—as quickly as possible. • Each speaker should wait for the previous idea to be charted before speaking. • It's OK to pass. • OK to build on previous ideas, but otherwise no critiquing or evaluating of ideas presented. • Complete three rounds of 20 seconds each. • Flip to the back of the chart pad for additional blank pages if needed. • If ideas are flowing, keep going, up to 10 minutes.	Up to 10 minutes

(Continued)

(Continued)

Action Plan	• Tear off all pages of brainstormed ideas and post on the walls. • Flip to the Action Plan page. • Facilitate a discussion of brainstormed ideas. What ideas should be included in the Action Plan? • Be sure to fill in all columns for each chosen idea that is listed under What.	10 minutes
Evidence of Success	• Flip to Evidence of Success page. • Facilitate a discussion of ways the team will be able to tell if the chosen actions are working, especially at the beginning stages.	5 minutes
Debriefing	• Discuss protocol itself. • How the process went • Whether time frames were adequate for each step • To what degree norms were followed • How this protocol might be used by teams in the school • Other ways the GC might use this protocol	2 minutes
Parking Lot	• As time allows, discuss any Parking Lot items.	

Adapted from Schmoker, M. (1999b). *Results: The key to continuous school improvement* (2nd ed., pp. 119–120). Used with permission from ASCD.

Suggested Materials and Equipment for Agenda

- Handouts, three-hole punched
  - Agenda
  - After Action Review
  - Planning/Problem Solving Protocol
  - Professional Work Plan and Team Commitments for individual note taking, as desired

- Signed Norms poster
- Roles/Responsibilities tent cards
- After Action Review enlarged to poster size
- Chart rack, markers, tape
- Chart pad on the chart stand, with pages already prepared with chart headers in the order of the protocol
- On the Action Plan page, draw vertical lines to separate the columns under What, By (when), and Who
- Talking Stick
- Poster size copy of agenda posted (or projected)
- Questions of a PLC enlarged to poster size
- Professional Work Plan and Team Commitments enlarged to poster size, including additional copies of page 2 to include all teams
- Parking Lot enlarged to poster size and hung in the meeting area
- Sticky notes, 3x3 inches or larger for potential Parking Lot items
- Tool Kit poster with running list of tools introduced

AGENDA NOTES ■

Planning/Problem Solving Protocol

If the Planning/Problem Solving Protocol is the first protocol you are bringing to the GC, consider choosing from the handouts from Chapter 9 as a general introduction to protocols.

For a problem-solving topic idea for simulating and/or practicing this protocol, choose a school-wide issue such as tardies, absences, or homework. Wording for a possible focusing question is: What can we do about all the students who _____?

The process will flow most smoothly if you have today's Recorder do the charting, while you act as Facilitator.

Tool Kit

The Planning/Problem Solving Protocol can be added to GC members' individual Tool Kits and the team's Tool Kit.

■ AFTER THE MEETING— PRINCIPAL FOLLOW UP SUGGESTIONS

Please refer to the Principal Follow Up Suggestions and Troubleshooting notes at the end of Chapter 10. If your team used this protocol for a real-life purpose that was not simply a simulation, be sure to ask an office staff member to take charge of the charts and to type up the Action Plan to be e-mailed to all GC members. Be sure to calendar any tasks from the Action Plan that you personally committed to fulfilling. Take whatever actions are possible to address leftover Parking Lot issues, or add them to the next GC meeting agenda.

■ TROUBLESHOOTING

Although introducing this protocol does not typically generate the kinds of concern and potential resistance that may occur with the Student Work Protocol and Student-Based Protocol, teachers still may voice concerns about whether all future team meetings will require the use of protocols. Consider referring back to some of the handouts from Chapter 9—which the teacher leaders may also be using with their team members—to help clarify the place of protocols in the overall picture of the developing work of teams. Reassure teachers that open discussions still have value and will continue to have a place in the teams' work.

■ SUMMARY

The Planning/Problem Solving Protocol (PPSP) can be adapted for a variety of uses. It is a high-energy discussion tool that often unleashes unexpected creativity in teams. Since teachers will not be sharing data or work samples, it can be a safe and successful choice for introducing protocols to the staff. In this agenda, you will facilitate the PPSP with the guiding coalition for an authentic planning or problem solving purpose, enabling GC members, in turn, to introduce it in their own teams.

Access links and additional resources at
www.corwin.com/sharedleadership

13

Guiding Coalition Meeting

Goal Setting and SMARTe Goals

You might wonder why goal setting is not introduced earlier, in the chapters on beginning team collaboration. If you feel strongly about this you should certainly pull the content of this meeting forward in your work with your team, but it is placed here for two reasons. First, it has been my experience that teams need time to simply gain proficiency in working together in what may be very new, more formalized ways than in the past. Second, once teams are ready to begin analyzing student data, having a baseline for measuring (the M in the acronym) student growth from one assessment to the next makes initial goal setting much easier. Until they have created/selected and then administered a couple of common assessments (see Chapters 5–6), they won't have any data to use as that baseline. This is not to say that teams cannot set a goal for an initial assessment, but when team goal setting is new, a baseline helps the process make sense, and the element of student growth adds a dimension of team motivation for setting and tracking goals.

It is essential that teams do begin setting common goals. This is the essence of teamwork in a school that is a professional learning community (PLC). Collaboration about improved instructional practices is a good way to increase collegiality, but in our age of accountability, this is not enough. Teams must be able to gauge student progress, and setting common goals ups the ante—it creates interdependency. Everyone must do their part for the team to make its goals. It also builds collective efficacy—the belief that all students can achieve outcomes of significance through teamwork. The notion that "all the students are everyone's students" grows from making and achieving common goals.

Finally, while short-cycle (i.e., weekly, monthly) common assessments are essential for accelerating student growth, other kinds of tasks, projects, and assignments are only given periodically. Some of these can also result in high-leverage discussions for teams if they set SMARTe goals at the outset of those units of instruction, even though there may not necessarily be a baseline score to use to set an improvement goal. These kinds of goals may read something like: At least 90 of our 100 students will attain at least a 3 on the 4-point rubric for the _____ project due April 1, including students learning English.

■ SMARTe AND S FOR SPECIFIC

SMART goals are now so well known that you probably will not need to spend much time with the guiding coalition (GC) on what the acronym represents, but it is worth a brief review. SMARTe was a variation that one cohort of teams agreed on for their own district. The added e was to remind team members that these goals should apply to *everyone*—each and every student. It is easy to fall into a habit of making general goals that result in certain students' needs and progress (or lack of it) being lost. Consider this: "Wow, we made our SMART goal! We set a goal for at least a 20% improvement, and we got 22%! Hooray!" What does this mean, exactly? First, we have to ask the team to unpack what the goal meant: Did the 20% increase refer to students, or scores? If it represented students, what did they have to do? What was the cut score, pass rate, grade, or other numeric measure the team was looking for? If the 20% improvement represented scores, how many students made this improvement? As you probably recall, the S in the acronym stands for Specific and Strategic. These considerations are all about the Specific part—what exactly do those numbers represent? Both students and scores are obviously important and should be clarified in the goal. In this case, whether it represented scores or students, you can see how easy it is to look at group averages and lose track of those students who chronically underperform. The SMARTe acronym challenges teams to set goals that include these students specifically so that during instructional planning, attention can be focused on accelerating their progress while maintaining upward momentum for the student group as a whole. This may entail setting multiple goals for the same assessment, with one of the goals targeting students on IEPs, for example.

■ S IS ALSO FOR STRATEGIC

Strategic goals are those that go after essential, enduring, high-leverage skills and concepts, as well as ambitious levels of improvement. In the latter case, working to get 5% more students to attain a pass rate is not very strategic, and even less strategic if the score to pass is low. Regarding skills and concepts, I wage an endless crusade with teams to choose higher-leverage skills for SMARTe goal setting than discrete, low-level ones like spelling, language conventions, and math facts. It is not that these skills are unimportant. But I do everything I can to discourage teams from expending their finite resources of the team's time, and their collective energy and expertise, setting these kinds of goals and collaborating around instruction for those purposes, especially on a long-term basis. Alone, they simply do not provide sufficient leverage to engineer improvement in student outcomes of significance. These low-level skills are examples of the many things for teachers to work on individually, after sharing a few ideas or selecting computer software from the team budget so the students can get more practice. It is impossible to collaborate about everything. Because collaboration time is so limited, teams must select the most vital, *strategic* goal areas on which to focus their collective expertise and energy.

M FOR MEASURABLE ■

Now that your teams have at least begun the practice of developing/selecting common assessments (which, remember, includes a range of assessment tools such as common assignments and performance tasks), they are ready for setting measurable goals. What is the baseline? For the most recent assessment, how did the team define student proficiency, mastery, or attainment of the objective? Then how many students demonstrated learning at that level? For next time, does the team wish to keep the cut score the same and work on the number of students who attain that level or to increase the attainment level as well as the number of students making it? And of course, don't forget the e; does the team need a separate goal, or an addendum to the main goal, for any specific group of students who are underperforming?

Finally, although SMART or SMARTe goals are traditionally set using percentages, I encourage you to consider having teams transition to using numbers of students. Why? SMART goals did not originate in education, but in the business world. Percentages are very efficient for measuring improvements in all kinds of business metrics, such as profits. But students are human beings, and I have found that asking teams to look at how many *students* a percentage represents is a game changer. Breakthroughs occur in creating meaning for the goal-setting process.

I first discovered this when I asked teams at schools in sanctions to convert state test score percentages to numbers of students. As a team discovered that they missed the cut point for proficiency at a particular grade level in mathematics or English language arts by, say, three students, it was a most startling revelation. "Three students! We missed it by *three students?? Who are they?*" As soon as that question surfaced, we had the breakthrough. Sometimes a team would say, "Wow, we only have three teachers who teach that! That means each teacher only needed to bump up one kid's performance." Since this returned the focus to the numbers game instead of thinking about specific students, my challenge was still to refocus the discussion on students. Nevertheless, all this was an entirely different conversation than the one about how to improve from X% to Y% proficiency.

We moved from the abstract to the concrete when teams thought of the numbers as students rather than percentages.

■ A FOR ATTAINABLE

No doubt you can see the overlap of Strategic and Attainable. The 5% improvement mentioned earlier is most likely entirely attainable, but usually this is not at all strategic. Setting a goal that challenges the team to do their best without being completely out of reach is the key to A. Some of your teachers have a coaching background—call that out. This team can be the underdogs, and win! And if they don't quite make it, regroup and make a new game plan.

■ R FOR RESULTS-ORIENTED

The goal must state exactly what the students will demonstrate. A SMARTe goal states an outcome, versus describing activities. "Students will study the Civil War" is a non-example. Results must be specified by the pass rate, cut score, rubric score, and so on; thus there is an overlap with S—the need to be specific.

■ T FOR TIME-BOUND

This is essentially the deadline for when the common assessment will be completed. SMARTe goals are not open-ended, although a unit or course of study might be. "By _____ (date) . . ." is a common way to begin a SMARTe goal.

■ SMARTe GOALS FOR COMPLEX OUTCOMES

The kinds of learning measured by the most recent assessments for both Common Core State Standards (CCSS) and non-CCSS states are quite different than what has been measured by standardized tests in the past. These are more substantive kinds of assessment. Many SMART goals have traditionally been written for measuring outcomes related to more traditional, standalone skills and fairly straightforward skill sets, although high levels of rigor were still possible.

As you and the GC move teams into writing SMARTe goals, I encourage you to shift as soon as possible from goals based on simple skill sets to those based on more complex learning. A good way to start is to introduce the wider use of rubrics for everyday instruction and assignments. At the secondary level, English teachers typically have a good handle on rubrics—consider tapping them, especially those who are GC members, for help in developing and presenting professional learning to the rest of the staff.

If rubrics are not widely used across the school, then as with any such new area that becomes apparent as a staff need, members of the guiding coalition—the Learning Leaders—are the logical ones to investigate, learn, try out, then present it to their colleagues. Conferences, district professional development, books, and the Internet are all possible sources for having GC members become experts-in-residence. The credibility teachers have with their own peers often results in much greater openness and learning among staff than would result from bringing in an outside guru.

SMARTe GOALS FOR VERTICAL TEAMS AND TEAMS OF SPECIALISTS ■

What about teams, such as vertical teams or specialists teams, that do not give common assessments? SMARTe goals can still be written using grades, writing prompts, or performance tasks written for subject-specific content but all graded on the same scale, such as a four-point scale. Regularly administered, school-wide assessments commonly used in elementary schools such as Dynamic Indicators of Basic Early Literacy Skills (DIBELS), reading probes, or running records are a strong basis for goal-based collaboration for elementary vertical teams. In schools moving closer to becoming highly effective professional learning communities, all teams write common goals. In a secondary team of specialists, the teachers of chorus, band, and drama might write a performance-based SMARTe goal, while the other members set a writing-based SMARTe goal for the same time period.

SMARTe GOALS AND DISCUSSION PROTOCOLS ■

How do SMARTe goals fit with discussion protocols? As the team leader develops the agenda, he or she may elect to either add the SMARTe goal discussion to the protocol steps or to make it a separate agenda item. The latter will usually be the most logical choice when the Student Work Protocol is used. If the team is going to use the Student-Based Protocol, it is logical to examine whether the goal was met at the beginning of the meeting, before Successes and Challenges are shared, than to set a new goal right before or right after Brainstorming.

I strongly recommend having team leaders collect and compile everyone's SMARTe goal data before the meeting, to avoid the time drain of charting this while the team meets. The team leader can either create a chart or simply make a handout showing each teacher's data and the overall team results.

Suggested Meeting Setup:

- Post the Questions of a PLC for reference
- Post the signed Norms poster

Agenda

Guiding Coalition Meeting

1. Review Norms and Assign Meeting Roles

2. Community Building

3. After Action Review

4. SMARTe Goals

5. Team Planning

6. Tool Kit

7. Evaluate Norms

Notes Page

S

M

A

R

T

e

Are These SMARTe Goals?

1. Improve seventh-grade student achievement in reading comprehension of informational text before our next monthly assessment, as measured by weekly student scores on homework passages.

2. Raise the pass rate of tenth graders in Geometry by 15%.

3. The number of third graders scoring at least 80% on monthly math problem solving assessments will improve from 29 out of 133 students on last month's quiz to at least 90 out of 133 students on next month's quiz, with at least half of our 14 students on IEPs scoring at least 80% on next month's quiz.

SMARTe Goal Worksheet

SMARTe Goal Period:

Assessment:

Goal score:

Baseline (if available):

Goal number of students:

SAMPLE

SMARTe Goal Period: October 3 to November 5

Assessment: Monthly math problem solving assessment

Goal score: 80%

Baseline: 29/133 October, including 2/14 students on IEPs

Goal number of students: 90/133 November, including 7/14 students on IEPs

Write a SMARTe Goal for These Teams

<u>Specialists Team (Arts/Career Tech)</u>: At the first progress report, the team has an average D–F rate of 31% for all sections.

<u>Fifth-Grade Team</u>: The team's students scored as follows on the first persuasive essay:

Rubric Score	# of Students
4	9
3	7
2	67
I	26*
	*Included all students on IEPs

Suggested Materials and Equipment for Agenda

- Handouts, three-hole punched

    o Agenda
    o After Action Review
    o Notes page
    o Are These SMARTe Goals?
    o SMARTe Goal Worksheet
    o Write a SMARTe Goal for These Teams
    o Professional Work Plan and Team Commitments for individual note taking, as desired

- Signed Norms poster
- Roles/Responsibilities tent cards
- After Action Review enlarged to poster size
- Chart rack, markers, tape
- Talking Stick
- Poster size copy of agenda posted (or projected)
- Questions of a PLC enlarged to poster size
- Professional Work Plan and Team Commitments enlarged to poster size, including additional copies of page 2 to include all teams
- Parking Lot enlarged to poster size and hung in the meeting area
- Sticky notes, 3x3 inches or larger for potential Parking Lot items
- Tool Kit poster with running list of tools introduced

AGENDA NOTES ■

SMARTe Goals

SMART goals are fairly widely used in schools, and the handouts for this meeting may be used either as an introduction or simply as a review for GC members. The added "e" for "everyone" serves as a reminder to ensure that every student is included in the goals.

If you use the handout Are These SMARTe Goals? you will note that some have components missing. The team may decide that some of the examples are incomplete in several ways, but at the very least, the first example does not provide the R—how results will be determined (SMAT goal)—what do the scores on these passages have to be? The second does not include the T—the time to evaluate the goal (SMAR goal)—does this refer to a monthly, semester, or annual evaluation of performance? The third goal, while wordy, does attempt to address all parts of the SMARTe goal.

For more detailed facilitation notes, please see the online resources on the companion website.

Tool Kit

SMARTe goals are now a tool GC members can add to their individual and the team's Tool Kit. The SMARTe Goal Worksheet is another tool they can use at any time with their teams to aid in developing their goals.

■ AFTER THE MEETING—PRINCIPAL FOLLOW UP SUGGESTIONS

You may be asked how often teams should (or must) use both SMARTe goals and protocols. If the team meets every week, should they use both every week? In my opinion, this would be overkill, but setting goals too infrequently—such as once a semester—makes it easy to lose sight of the continuous energy that needs to be applied toward achieving the goal, especially if it is a strategic, challenging goal as it should be. Every 3 to 4 weeks seems to be a good rule of thumb for developing or selecting a high-leverage common assessment and setting a goal to see tangible, ongoing improvement in student outcomes. Once a team is comfortable using SMARTe goals, it only adds a few minutes to their meeting to evaluate the past one and develop a new one. The point of all teamwork is to improve student learning. Encourage teams to use protocols—and eventually write their own—as often as needed to keep discussions on track and maximize the limited time teams have to meet. Protocols are the bridge from meetings-as-usual to high-level collaboration. SMARTe goals should remain in place for all teams, even those who seem to have moved past the need for protocols. Without goals, the need for interdependence is greatly diminished, if not eliminated—and without interdependence, a group of individuals is not a team.

■ SUMMARY

This agenda introduces or reviews SMARTe goals—the added e for "everyone." You will facilitate a review of the components of SMARTe goals, and GC members will have the opportunity to analyze written goals to determine if components are missing and practice writing new goals in this format.

Access links and additional resources at
www.corwin.com/sharedleadership

14

Building Shared Knowledge About Student Interventions

At times, so much attention is focused on teacher collaboration that it is easy to forget that this is not the only aspect of the school culture that sets a professional learning community (PLC) apart from a traditional school. In some schools, teacher teams or their meetings are referred to as *PLCs*, which may contribute to the neglect of other important aspects of the school's PLC development. To be sure, a grade-level or course-alike team can become a PLC even if the school is not; however, the ideal is for the school itself to become a PLC.

One such potentially neglected area is student interventions, sometimes called the Pyramid of Interventions, Response to Intervention (RTI), Pyramid Response to Intervention, or another term such as Multi-Tier System of Supports (MTSS). Whatever the term, the lack of a highly systematic, systemic, flexible, school-wide structure of student interventions creates an impervious ceiling on teachers' and teams' ability to accomplish outcomes of significance for every student.

■ TWO TRADITIONS THAT DO NOT SERVE STUDENTS

Traditionally, student interventions were often conducted—or offered—after school. Unfortunately, the students who most need interventions are the most unlikely to choose to stay after school for extra support. Bus schedules, family demands, and extracurricular activities also interfere with students' after school availability. Student interventions must be an integral part of the students' hours of regular attendance. It is also essential that interventions are conducted during the contract day when teachers can provide them, since paraprofessionals and volunteers cannot provide the necessary level of expertise for the neediest students. Alterations to time-honored schedules, like the bell schedule, bus schedule, and master schedule—painful as they may be—are often essential to ensure that no students are able to fall through the cracks.

A second unfortunate tradition was for teachers who had failing students to refer them for special education, resulting in what was typically a life sentence in a restrictive placement that limited the learning and success options for large numbers of students. Related to this tradition, in too many cases, the base of the pyramid—best first instruction, coupled with in-class interventions—was not in place. Thus, RTI was conceived with the notion of helping ensure that classroom instruction was extremely well-designed and delivered, keeping these students in mind; with in-class interventions provided as soon as any student began to struggle, the effects of the interventions analyzed and other strategies tried if those failed. In RTI, this is followed by successive tiers of more intensive strategies inside and outside

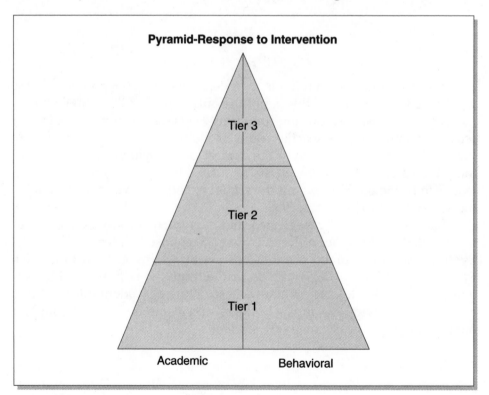

the classroom, often with the assistance of other staff and specialists—systematically designed, implemented, and analyzed—before special education referral is ever considered.

Interpreting the Pyramid

The pyramid structure represents the notion that once the teacher has attempted all suggested classroom-level strategies at the base (Tier 1), with high fidelity to their design, and the student still struggles, Tier 2 interventions are initiated—serving fewer students, thus the pyramid's tiers become progressively smaller. In a school that is a PLC, team-level interventions are an important component of Tier 2, but an array of other in-school interventions are also needed to provide a full safety net for students. Tier 3, the tip of the pyramid, represents the point at which the fewest students are served, in the most intense interventions. Student groupings are very small, sometimes even one-to-one. Interventions are of longer duration than in the lower tiers, but *Tier 3 does not imply permanent placement* in an intervention. Students who are still unsuccessful in Tier 3 are sometimes referred for special education placement.

When RTI and Pyramid of Interventions were entering the jargon of educators, I once observed a group of high school teachers respond to a presentation on interventions with, "Great! Pyramid of Interventions! Where am I sending all these kids who can't do anything in my class, and when are they going?" Obviously there was work to be done in creating understanding about the meaning of the levels of the pyramid, especially the pyramid's base. Classroom instruction in this particular department was overwhelmingly delivered whole-group, in a daily lecture format, with little or no scaffolding or differentiation. The reteaching loop was notably missing. At any school where such misunderstandings persist, a comprehensive system is clearly not in place, and understanding and creating the solid base of the pyramid is foundational to building the rest.

STUDENT NEEDS ARE COMPLEX ■

Often, teams succumb to the temptation to look at student interventions too simplistically. They are drawn to consider interventions for one category of students, on a single dimension: those who lack academic skills to perform successfully in the standards for their subject, grade, or grade span. In reality, young human beings are far more complex. Academic preparedness is only one dimension of the issues that cause students to be at risk in our education system. Motivation, effort, and attitude—a combination of factors that becomes increasingly apparent with age—interact with scholastic readiness to create a multifaceted array of considerations. Various aspects of the student's life outside of school, including mental and physical health, family and home conditions, and peer influences, may underlie an apparent lack of motivation and effort and/or negative attitudes.

To provide a fuller picture of student needs, a more helpful way to think of the pyramid structure is represented by the vertical line drawn from the tip to the base, as shown. One side is typically labeled the Academic side, the other the Behavioral side. The tiers on both sides represent increasing intensity of interventions, serving increasingly fewer students.

What is offered in the GC meeting agenda in Chapter 15 as a possible beginning step to creating a comprehensive system of student interventions is simply that: a beginning step. Developing your system will require much more time and energy than one meeting with your guiding coalition. However, many schools are far beyond this stage, and if your school is one of them, I invite you to consider what next steps you can take to share leadership with your teacher leaders in continuously refining and maintaining it, perhaps drawing on some of the References and Resources.

■ PRACTICES THAT ARE NOT INTERVENTIONS

Before you schedule the GC meeting to implement the agenda for beginning work on your school's system of interventions, you should consider scheduling one or more additional GC meetings beforehand to build shared knowledge with your teacher leaders, depending on what has historically been in place at your school. Vestiges of several practices, which were long considered *interventions*, but actually have very harmful effects, may still remain. It is important to avoid mistakenly augmenting them when you and your team begin working on your school-wide system of interventions. They are: ability grouping (the "robins, bluebirds, and buzzards" of yesteryear), tracking (honors track, average track, remedial track, college prep track, etc.), and grade retention, which is most commonly practiced at the elementary level but can be found through Grade 8 in some schools. The case against each of these practices based on research findings is immense.

If any of these practices remain in your school, use Google Scholar to cull articles—or invite your teacher leaders to do so—about them. As of this writing, here is a partial representation of the wealth of resources available to you to build this body of shared knowledge about practices that are NOT interventions:

1. Ability grouping

   Google Scholar hits on search for School Ability Grouping: 450,000

2. Tracking

   Google Scholar hits on search for School Tracking: 2,180,000

3. Grade retention

   Google Scholar hits on search for School Grade Retention: 651,000

The main purpose of building this body of shared knowledge at this particular time is to avoid growing any of these practices that remain in place at your school by mistakenly adding to them. Dismantling them completely will most likely require careful planning. Grade retention amounts to a sacred cow in some elementary schools, particularly at the kindergarten level. Many kindergarten teachers have never been provided with the research on grade retention and sincerely believe that retaining students (ironically, with a different teacher the second time) helps them. I have observed kindergarten teachers break down and cry, genuinely grieving when their schools or districts have begun moving toward policies prohibiting grade retention. As discussed in Chapter 8, this obviously represents second order change for these teachers. At the secondary level, dismantling a tracking system holds similar second order implications.

Shared leadership is never more important than in leading changes like these. For a principal to unilaterally abolish cherished practices—in spite of the fact that they are harmful to student learning—is to create a backlash that can defeat the most honorable of intended changes. Some teacher leaders in the guiding coalition may themselves have strong beliefs about the value of these practices, so a crucial beginning step is to create shared knowledge about them, using the research.

SO WHAT *SHOULD* WE DO? ■

A second step in creating shared knowledge is to examine research and examples of best practices for what student interventions *should* look like. General, global approaches such as a study skills class or a period where students work in grammar workbooks are not effective as interventions, because they are not targeted to each individual student's needs. Interventions need to be intensive, short-term, and tailored to *exactly* the skill or concept the student just missed. It is beyond the scope of this book to present the range and depth of material this topic deserves, but resources for planning effective interventions abound (see the References and Resources for a few of them). With the advent of RTI, the expertise of specialists has become more effectively applied to support general education teachers. Their ideas, coupled with team suggestions during regular collaboration, can bolster Tier 1 tremendously, which may have already begun to happen at your school.

Tier 2 should also include a variety of interventions, including supports provided by the collaborative team. One example of a simple Tier 2 team intervention is Remediation/Enrichment Days (REDs). The team designates a weekly or biweekly day for REDs. Students who did well on the most recent team assessment—which measured an essential, enduring, high-leverage (Strategic!) set of skills and knowledge—are divided among the teachers who will provide a period of enrichment. The rest are divided among the other teachers for *highly specific reteaching*. This is not a generalized study skills class or homework catch-up, but laser-like targeted instruction in the skills the students were unable to demonstrate. It makes sense for the teachers who had the best results on the assessment to work with the remedial students on that particular RED.

At the secondary level, this means that all the teachers who teach the same course during the same period (e.g., Algebra I, first period) share students for REDs. Shared leadership is important to help teams work out viable alternatives and logistical issues, such as classrooms that are not physically clustered together or a teacher who is the only one during a particular period teaching the course. At the elementary level, the teachers simply agree on a day of the week and a time frame.

While Tier 3 does not represent permanent placement in an intervention, its interventions are more intensive and last longer than those in Tiers 1 and 2. Specialized reading programs for secondary students, designed to accelerate them to within 2 years of grade level within a short period, are one example. It is very important to realize that there is *no* silver-bullet program in existence that a school can purchase to fix all student learning problems. Any program or approach must be carefully researched and examined before being selected, then carefully fitted into its niche in a particular tier of the overall system of school-wide interventions. The What Works Clearinghouse is a source for research-based programs that may be appropriate for a specific need in your system of interventions.

In the event that a decision is made to purchase any specialized program, a related, critical consideration is what it will take to implement the program as designed. Otherwise, instead of an intense intervention where students exit in a relatively short period, the program itself becomes an indeterminate sentence to be served. Common mistakes include assigning long-term substitutes or first-year teachers to teach the programs or assigning it to teachers who have classroom management problems or issues with student relationships. Another is to ignore the specifications for the program. For example, Read 180 is designed for a daily 90-minute period of instruction. Schools that have simply assigned the class to a 50-minute period never develop a track record of success with students, because it is impossible to implement all parts of the program, and all the parts are designed to work together to support accelerated improvement. A third error is to fail to provide professional learning and coaching in the program for its teachers. The publishers of programs like Read 180 provide intensive, multiday training and follow up, without which it is next to impossible for the teacher to master and implement the program successfully.

While I do not necessarily advocate the purchase of any sort of programs for Tier 3, they are sometimes highly successful as *part* of the school's Tier 3 interventions, but only if (1) they are staffed with the most excellent teachers, (2) implemented in strict accordance with their design, and (3) if the teachers receive the necessary professional learning and follow up to implement. As mentioned earlier, making modifications to the master schedule—to create a 90-minute period of instruction, for example—usually represents a change of second order proportions.

■ STEALTHY INTERVENTIONS

In *Stratosphere: Integrating Technology, Pedagogy, and Change Knowledge,* Michael Fullan (2013) discusses the intriguing idea of "stealthy interventions." See online resources for a short article explaining this approach, entitled Stealthy Interventions.

■ POSITIVE BEHAVIOR INTERVENTIONS AND SUPPORTS (PBIS)

Implementing PBIS enables schools to analyze the school climate as experienced by students, identify problem areas, and put structures in place at the campus and classroom level to reduce and eliminate discipline problems. It is student focused and has great potential for making the behavioral side of your Pyramid Response to Intervention more systematic and robust. Many resources can be found at www.pbis.org, the website of the

Technical Assistance Center on Positive Behavioral Interventions and Supports, established by the U.S. Department of Education's Office of Special Education Programs. But do not be misled; PBIS is for all students, not just for those in special education.

TIMING ■

As principal, your good judgment is key when considering when the time is right to broach another initiative. It is a fatal mistake to wait until "everyone is ready to get on board," because it is extremely unlikely that *everyone* will *ever* be ready. Having the courage to move anyway, in the face of some likely resistance, is inevitably necessary. For any change to be successful, teachers themselves must take ownership, and your GC teacher leaders are the vanguard of your staff. As you approach the work of developing your school's system of interventions, shared decision making with your GC leaders is critical for deciding on the timing to begin, how to create demand for the changes as discussed in Chapter 8, and for crafting the initial steps. Continue to use shared leadership to diligently monitor both early and continuing markers of student success, and the impact of the changes on the staff. Do not be afraid of making adjustments—they are necessary to work out the inevitable glitches—but do not simply abandon the initiative. And always begin with building shared knowledge as a community of professionals, learning together.

SUMMARY ■

A system of student interventions is foundational to a school's ability to function as a PLC. Replacing ineffective practices, such as offering interventions after school or creating a study skills class, with in-school, immediate, individual, targeted assistance requires careful planning. Eliminating harmful practices such as tracking, ability grouping, and grade-level retention may be even more complex because teachers may be unaware of their damage. Building shared knowledge with your GC about effective and ineffective practices is essential so that a robust system of interventions can be developed through shared leadership.

Access links and additional resources at
www.corwin.com/sharedleadership

15

Guiding Coalition Meeting

Student Interventions

Y ou have now spent whatever time was needed to build shared knowledge with your guiding coalition (GC) leaders about student interventions, and you are ready to hold a meeting with your GC to begin or continue working on your own school's system. At the beginning stages of developing systemic interventions, I use the following graphic with school teams to initiate a conversation about the needs of their students in a particular grade level or subject area. However, this general first look for the purposes of beginning to develop a school-wide system of interventions is never intended to suggest that it is a substitute for a unit-by-unit, skill-by-skill assessment of student needs that is a part of routine team collaboration.

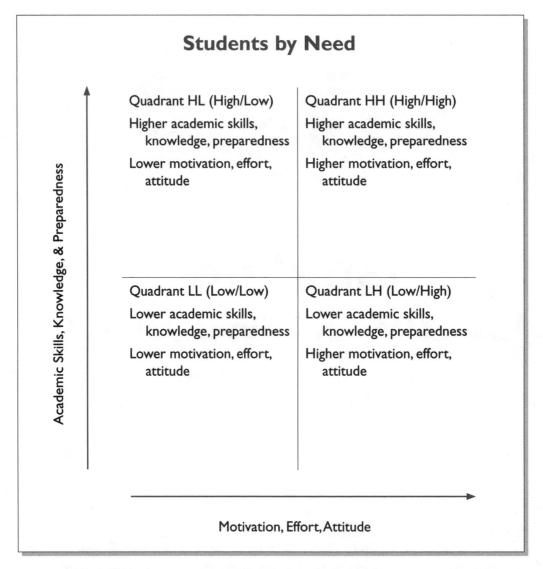

Students by Need

Quadrant HL (High/Low)

Higher academic skills, knowledge, preparedness

Lower motivation, effort, attitude

Quadrant HH (High/High)

Higher academic skills, knowledge, preparedness

Higher motivation, effort, attitude

Quadrant LL (Low/Low)

Lower academic skills, knowledge, preparedness

Lower motivation, effort, attitude

Quadrant LH (Low/High)

Lower academic skills, knowledge, preparedness

Higher motivation, effort, attitude

Academic Skills, Knowledge, & Preparedness

Motivation, Effort, Attitude

Before introducing this graphic with the four quadrants, I ask all the teachers on the team to individually complete alternate rankings of their students. This requires that each team member bring a class roster to the session. I ask secondary teachers to select a roster for only one class period—one that has a mix of high, middle, and low performing students. Before beginning, I ask the elementary teachers to choose either language arts or mathematics as their focus for the exercise.

To complete an alternate ranking, the teacher numbers a blank page from 1 to 30 (or whatever number the class enrollment is), then in ping-pong fashion lists the highest performing student, then the lowest performing, then the second-highest performing, and the next-to-lowest performing, and so on. To get the most accurate list, two things are important. One is to avoid the temptation to list students in order from top to bottom, and instead to continue in ping-pong fashion until every student is listed; the other is to complete it as quickly as possible, going with the gut reaction and not over-thinking it.

Once everyone has completed the alternate ranking, I ask the teachers to draw a horizontal line under the name of the last student who is consistently performing at grade level or at course expectations. Thus, those below the line consistently perform below grade-level/course expectations.

Note that all this is completed without grade books, grades, or assessment results; it is simply a reflection of teachers' subjective assessment of the day-to-day performance of students in their classes and works very well for the purpose of this session.

Once the quadrant graphic is distributed, we spend a few minutes discussing and clarifying the differences in the four sets of descriptions. Then I ask each teacher to write the first name of each student on the alternate ranking in the quadrant that best represents what he or she believes is behind that student's typical performance.

As we debrief the exercise, several valuable insights emerge. The major aha is that the observable symptom of low performance in an individual student can have a variety of causes and combinations of causes, not all of which are academic. Another is that, not surprisingly, most teachers can readily fill in the very top performing and lowest performing students, but slow down considerably when they get to the middle. Without the class rosters, many say they would be unable to complete the alternate ranking. A conclusion teachers typically draw from this is that as educators, we pay lots of attention to both ends of the performance spectrum, possibly neglecting the needs of many students in between, all the while—ironically— "teaching to the middle."

Another insight is that students' performance fluctuates, and the teacher may not have much certainty about why. I hear, "Well, sometimes he . . . but at other times he . . ." Typically, more than one teacher will say, "I wanted to write [his/her] name right on the dividing line." This insight is particularly important, because it helps teams avoid the pitfall of mistaking practices like traditional classroom ability grouping for an intervention: One of the most critical features of interventions is flexibility, both in student groupings and in the time frames for the interventions to run. As the content changes, each student will have different skill gaps and other varying needs.

Meeting Preparation

Ask the office manager to e-mail all GC members and ask them to each bring a class roster to the meeting. Secondary teachers should bring a class roster for one period or section, selecting a class with students whose typical performance spans a range of high, medium, and low.

Suggested Meeting Setup:

- Post the Questions of a PLC for reference
- Post the signed Norms poster

Agenda

Guiding Coalition Meeting

1. Review Norms and Assign Meeting Roles

2. Community Building

3. After Action Review

4. Student Interventions

5. Team Planning

6. Tool Kit

7. Evaluate Norms

Alternate Ranking

1. Number a lined or blank sheet of paper up to the number of students in your class or section—for example, 1–30 for a class of 30.

2. List the name of the student who typically is top performing in the class on Line 1. List the name of the student whose performance is typically at the bottom on Line 30 (or whatever the last line is).

3. Next, list the name of the student who is typically the #2 performer on Line 2, and then the student who is #29 on Line 29.

4. Refer to your class roster as needed to ensure that all names are listed.

5. Continue in this fashion until all students are listed.

6. Draw a line under the name of the last student who consistently performs at grade level or at course expectations. Those below the line will be those who consistently perform below those expectations.

Avoid

- Listing names in order from 1–30. Ping-pong fashion between top and bottom yields more accurate and useful results.
- Over-thinking. Go with your "gut reaction" and list names as quickly as possible.

Suggested Materials and Equipment for Agenda

- Handouts, three-hole punched

  - Agenda
  - After Action Review
  - Alternate Ranking
  - Students by Need
  - Professional Work Plan and Team Commitments for individual note taking, as desired

- Class rosters (brought by each teacher)
- Blank or lined paper
- Pyramid Response to Intervention graphic from Chapter 14, enlarged to poster size
- Mini Avery dots (optional)
- Signed Norms poster
- Roles/Responsibilities tent cards
- After Action Review enlarged to poster size
- Chart rack, markers, tape
- Talking Stick
- Poster size copy of agenda posted (or projected)
- Questions of a PLC enlarged to poster size
- Professional Work Plan and Team Commitments enlarged to poster size, including additional copies of page 2 to include all teams
- Parking Lot enlarged to poster size and hung in the meeting area
- Sticky notes, 3x3 inch or larger for potential Parking Lot items
- Tool Kit poster with running list of tools introduced

AGENDA NOTES ■

Student Interventions

If you have GC members complete the Alternate Ranking, it works best to have elementary teachers select either English language arts or mathematics as their focus. It is helpful to have the Alternate Ranking completed before using the Students by Need handout. Teachers can write the first names only of each of their students in one of the four quadrants.

I debrief this by asking the Recorder to title a blank chart page: What We Noticed. Then I invite team members to share insights from this process while the Recorder charts them. In the process, I elicit discussions of the following if they do not emerge from team members:

- A variety of factors may interfere with learning—some academic, some nonacademic. It is typically easy to name the most able and most needy students; those in the midrange are harder to remember—and to focus on when teaching and planning.
- A given student's academic abilities and nonacademic factors, such as motivation, can vary considerably from one class to another and one unit to another.

- Information about some students may be incomplete; teachers may not have background information—for example, regarding home, health, peers—which may be impacting learning.

Once the insights have been charted, we post it nearby, then we use the Pyramid Response to Intervention poster. I ask the Recorder to draw the horizontal tier lines across the full page to allow more room to write ideas for each tier on both sides of the pyramid.

I recommend using the Brainstorming guidelines from Chapter 12, 123 to facilitate a short, intense, high-energy brainstorming session around the six areas of the pyramid. Remember that every idea is captured, with no critiquing of its merit or feasibility. It works best to begin at the base, beginning with Academic Tier 1, then moving to Behavioral Tier 1, then moving on to Tier 2 and repeating the two sides in alternating fashion.

If the meeting space allows, post the chart pages from the brainstorming so that they all can be seen by all team members.

Use appropriate tools, such as the Talking Stick if emotions are high, and fist-to-five consensus building as needed as you decide which ideas to pursue during Team Planning. Be sure the charts themselves are stored in an accessible place for future reference. Using Avery dots as described in Chapter 6 is another strategy you can use to help prioritize the agreed-upon slate of selected ideas to implement.

Remember to consider resources such as nearby schools that have implemented successful interventions. Professional field trips are a useful tool.

During Team Planning, the team may also decide to use a staff professional learning session to have teachers complete their own alternate rankings and list their students in the Students by Need quadrants for group discussion.

Tool Kit

The Alternate Ranking and Students by Need quadrants are tools GC members can use at any time with their teams and can now be added to members' individual Tool Kits and the team Tool Kit.

■ AFTER THE MEETING— PRINCIPAL FOLLOW UP SUGGESTIONS

Your involvement with teams as they put Tier 2 academic and behavioral interventions in place is a critical support. Symbolically, it will emphasize the importance of developing these interventions, and your ability to balance your leadership between stepping up by providing answers and ideas, and stepping back to coach, guide, and question your teams to push their thinking, will be essential to their success.

Take time to reflect on the needs of individual teachers on your staff for Tier 1. How many of them still need support and/or accountability to ensure that their students truly receive BEST first instruction? What do they each need—additional professional learning, individual coaching from an academic coach, smaller steps of implementation, increased support from teammates during collaboration, more administrative accountability? Do any teachers have classroom management problems? If so, their students do not have a solid base in the academic side of the pyramid at Tier 1. What do you need to do to ensure that they improve?

What action steps did you commit to fulfilling in the Professional Work Plan regarding school-wide interventions for Tiers 2 and 3? What support do the teacher leaders need who committed to fulfilling action steps?

Building and maintaining your Pyramid Response to Intervention is a continuous work in progress. It is never finished, because student needs will change. If interventions are not maintained through continuously ensuring support of the staff who provide them, they will fade away or lose their effectiveness because they have lost consistency, student progress monitoring, or rigor. Are there teachers in addition to those on the guiding coalition who are ready to step up to leadership roles in this area? How about support staff? Can the office staff help with facilitating workflow and communication about specific students moving through the system of interventions? Since adding to the number of balls you need to personally juggle and keep aloft will be unlikely to pave the way for success, consider how you can share leadership to maintain and continuously evaluate the tiers of your pyramid.

SUMMARY ■

The agenda for this GC meeting assumes that you have built shared knowledge about effective and ineffective practices with your teacher leaders as discussed in the previous chapter. This agenda employs a grid termed Students by Need and a strategy known as Alternate Ranking for GC members to first consider the needs of the students they personally teach. These results provide a starting point for discussions to design a full system of interventions encompassing all tiers of the RTI Pyramid, with both academic and behavioral considerations.

 Access links and additional resources at
www.corwin.com/sharedleadership

16

Guiding Coalition Meeting

Working With Challenging Individuals

Y ou may have skipped directly to this chapter when you saw it in the Table of Contents. This meeting—or elements of it—can be used at any point in the sequence of guiding coalition (GC) meetings as you personalize them for your school and your teacher leaders.

To some readers, it may seem that discussions in this book about individuals who have difficulty with change stem from a belief that schools are filled with teachers who care more about their own needs, comfort, and convenience than the needs of students, adamantly resist change, and frequently behave in an unprofessional manner. Nothing could be further from the truth. However, having even one individual on a team who appears to fit this description looms large as a barrier. As discussed in Chapter 8, such behaviors are often fear based, but regardless of the cause, over time, such a teacher may have developed a powerful and intimidating persona, consistently brought to bear whenever change is introduced to protect the status quo. Certain traditional features of schools perpetuate the development of these personae, including teacher isolation and autonomy, a possible history of administrative reluctance to deal with unprofessional behavior and interpersonal issues among staff, and relationships between teachers and administrators that are historically adversarial. For a teacher leader working to lead a team with one or more such peers, it is a daunting mission. Another tradition that exacerbates challenges in the move toward developing teacher leadership is what Roland Barth (2013) refers to as a *taboo*: "There's also a taboo in our profession against one teacher elevating himself or herself above the others. You see it with merit-pay discussions, but you also see it when one teacher takes responsibility for something in the school and the other teachers are just worrying about their own 30 kids. The teacher who takes a leadership role can expect to be punished by fellow teachers" (p. 10).

Perhaps in your school, *punished* is an overly strong word for what your teacher leaders may be feeling. In others, when all the factors mentioned above have become fortified with time, cultures have developed that can only be described as toxic. As the principal, changing such a culture can only begin with you. Prior principals' laissez faire style may have resulted in the development of the culture, so you must be very proactive to change it. An education leadership student I once had in a master's class wrote in her paper, "My principal doesn't use any of the [leadership] approaches described in our text, unless I missed the avoidance approach." An elementary principal I worked with, when confronted with teachers' inappropriate behaviors, or interpersonal issues—including serious ones—among the mostly female staff, referred to them as "a bunch of squabbling women" and steadfastly refused to involve himself.

Debbie Fay, now HR Director in the Moreno Valley Unified School District, became the principal of a middle school that fell into state sanctions soon after she arrived. She often referred to her staff as a whole as "the silent majority," but she had a number of highly vocal, negative teachers who had held sway over their colleagues for many years. Prior administrators had simply turned a blind eye to the staff interpersonal dynamics, allowing a culture to develop where students and families were blamed for failure, with members of the silent majority bullied into remaining silent. Staff meetings and department meetings were dominated by this small group of teachers, who fed off each other's negative energy in any group setting. Course-alike teaming had never been attempted. Through a steady, persistent process of developing teacher leaders and teacher ownership of the school's improvement steps, relentlessly confronting negativity wherever she encountered it, and making clear that unprofessional behavior would not be tolerated, Debbie led her school out of sanctions, and the school became a model of teacher collaboration and in-school student supports and interventions, hosting visitors from all over California. It is a testament to her strength in developing shared leadership that she always maintained, "I didn't do this. We did it."

Your GC members are the ones on the line, day in and day out, placed in a possibly new leadership role that may or may not be welcomed by their teammates. Even on teams whose members are normally positive, the normal stresses of teaching take their toll on everyone and may emerge unexpectedly in resistance to yet another phase in the change process. Teacher leaders must not only step up to internalize each change personally, but then also are called on to support their teammates in the change. This is a significant demand and requires principal diligence in staying sensitive and attuned to their needs and to supporting them in their developing roles of leadership.

The contents of this chapter and its GC meeting agenda will make more sense if you first review Chapter 8: Managing Complex Change. Understanding the research on what makes change difficult for individuals will help you and your GC members manage personal transitions for colleagues who are resisting or struggling with change.

As discussed in Chapter 8, using arguments or logic is usually futile in the effort to change someone's mind or philosophy. It is only through *experiencing* something different than what we expect that we are forced to rethink our beliefs. Only administrators can *require* individuals to behave in a new way and thus have a new experience, such as attending team collaborations, arriving on time and prepared, and behaving professionally. Team leaders cannot *require* any of these things of their peers, although having norms and other routines and procedures in place will help team leaders lead teams with challenging members. It is through the gradual experiencing of new ways of interacting that these resistant team members can begin to change. But during that gradual process, team leaders can easily become discouraged and tempted to give up on their colleagues.

A UNITED FRONT ■

One of the subtleties that can sabotage the best work of leadership teams is the communication of inconsistent messages from team members when confronted with peer negativity. Consider the following scenario:

It is early morning—around 7:15 a.m.—and Joseph, a GC member, is at the staff mailboxes getting his mail. Marie, a powerful and highly negative veteran teacher, pulls the weekly staff bulletin from her mailbox and bursts out, "Gimme a break! First, we have to attend these WORTHLESS team meetings, and NOW we have to bring our own classes' results for everyone to see?!! Who in the #$@% thought this up?!!"

She turns a glaring eye to Joseph—many years Marie's junior in age as well as years at the school—who mumbles something like, "Mmm. This might be really moving too fast. Yeah, mmm, you're probably right."

As soon as Marie marches off, Joseph knows he has made a mistake, and indeed, at every opportunity for the rest of the day, Marie announces triumphantly to all within earshot, "Hey, even our ILLUSTRIOUS Guiding Coalition thinks we're 'moving too fast'" (mimicking Joseph).

In a profession where the cultural legacy of over 100 years stands insistently against teachers' stepping into leadership roles, how can you protect your teacher leaders from this kind of emotional assault, as well as protect your fledgling initiatives for students from emerging DOA?

Part of the answer is the development of a clearly articulated united front, and another is the courage of the principal to relentlessly address this kind of negativity—wherever it arises—as professionally unacceptable.

It is essential that each teacher leader—and every other staff member who has begun to take ownership of shared leadership to improve learning for all students—presents a consistent response to the kinds of comments typical of the Maries on staff. That is the emphasis of this GC meeting. A growing tide of positive peer resistance to negaholics will become much more powerful than administrative intervention for reducing their ability to control and intimidate others, BUT administrative intervention is sometimes not simply necessary but essential. It is absolutely critical that the principal communicates and puts teeth into the standard that spiteful, negative comments that do not contribute to a productive dialog about change are unacceptable. How do you put teeth into this? By consistently addressing individuals in the instances—in a scrupulously respectful manner, always in a private setting—when they insist on continuing to behave in this way.

■ THE "PROFESSIONAL EXCUSE"

I think that one of the most interesting ways that resistors couch their resistance is to use what I've come to think of as the Professional Excuse. It goes something like this: We are so busy doing a great job and working hard for our students, we just don't have any extra time or energy right now for changing what we do—maybe next year? I have also seen principals, unfortunately, buy into this—it seems so logical, so caring, so, well, professional. When I hear this approach, I will confess that usually my first thought is that rearranging the deck chairs on the *Titanic*—no matter how fervent or even feverish—is not a useful or honorable activity, but my response is usually something about data. "Wow, really? I didn't realize your data was so strong! Let's take a look. Do you have a minute?" For this purpose, the teacher's data can be any indicator of student success and progress, including grades (which can be particularly telling), short cycle assessment results, benchmark scores, even state test scores. Drawing the connection for the teacher between the work of her team, which she is resisting, and its expected result in supporting her in making continuous improvements in her instruction for the success of each and every student is at the heart of this conversation.

Related to this, Richard DuFour wrote a pointed, very brief article published in 2007, which remains as timely as ever, titled "We're Already a 'Good' School; Why Do We Have to Improve?" I have found it quite useful in my beginning work with teams at some schools. To read the article online, search for the title in a search engine. Or find the live link on the companion website under Resource Articles and Videos.

■ "YOU'RE STARTING TO SOUND LIKE AN ADMINISTRATOR!"

It is a sad commentary on the education profession that these words are intended—and often felt—to be a kind of ultimate insult when directed from one teacher to another. When I broach this with leadership teams, I sometimes project an image of Darth Vader with this statement printed beneath it. Teachers moving into administrative positions are sometimes jokingly reminded by both colleagues and administrative mentors that they are "going over to the dark side." We might well wonder how we arrived at a point where this abyss between teachers and administrators is so pronounced in some districts and schools. Reaching and teaching all students is a huge challenge, with many difficult moments. How is it that we are not all on the same side?

In Leaders' Link, a weekly online leadership column for HotChalk, Inc., I once wrote a piece on this very topic. It is reprinted here with permission.

Teachers vs. Administrators: Ending the Adversarial Relationship

An administrative colleague of mine recently retired from the school where she'd worked for many years, and wrote a farewell open letter to her staff. As part of a warm, positive goodbye, she said:

> Over the years, [our school] redefined itself. Teachers began to trust and work together to accomplish great things. As more and more teachers took leadership roles in school site council, leadership team, and the restructuring team, they came to trust "the administration." So now I am going to be a bit preachy. I have stated it to some, but now I state it to all: those words are insulting and hurtful. They imply division, us-against-them, and manipulation or coercion. At least, when I hear those words, that is generally the [implication]. Most administrators have a solid history as teachers, association reps, and advocates for children. However, once assigned to an administrative position, too often all the background experience and empathy is lost in perception. I urge you to get to know your administrative partners before casting judgment and all too easily referring to those dedicated people as "the administration." You have reached extraordinary heights of excellence due to teachers, students, parents, staff and administrators. It is a true partnership and villainy is not helpful.

As I reflected on this section of the letter, I wished that all teachers who disparagingly refer to "the administration" at their sites could read it.

Labeling Teachers as Troublemakers

Similarly, another colleague of mine—a newer administrator, who was the former, long standing president of her district's teachers' union—attended a multiday professional development series for administrators that I facilitated. In one session, I was guilty of making several stereotypical remarks about unions and union reps based on years of negative experiences in two former districts where I worked as a site- and district-level administrator.

While most of the group was nodding their heads, my colleague took me to task—very appropriately and respectfully—both publicly when I made these remarks and privately later. She reminded me that too often teachers who raise questions to their administrators about new initiatives, especially if they make reference to the contract, are quickly branded as troublemakers and treated in a very dismissive manner thereafter. This reaction is both undeserved and obstructive to positive change for students.

I was grateful for her courage, and her willingness to challenge my perspective. As I talked through my experiences with her, I found it ironic to also recall that as a teacher I had been a union rep myself for several years and an active union committee member for several more.

Toward a True Partnership:
Tips for Teachers and Administrators

It is imperative that we end the adversarial relationship between teachers and administrators if we are to reach the goal of ensuring that all students graduate from our systems fully prepared for college and the global workforce. Thus, I offer the following suggestions:

For teachers:

- Catch yourself before stereotyping administrators in general and yours in particular. Trust is a two-way street. To improve trust, you have to participate, and a good place to begin is to stop yourself when these reactions arise automatically.
- Use administrators' personal names with their titles (Mr. Smith, Dr. Jones), or better yet, their first names (Don, Donna) instead of just saying "Smith" or "Jones." This will make the person more human, both to you and to others.
- Presume positive intentions for students; do not presume negative intentions for staff. This is a tough one, because as my friend's letter pointed out, we tend to malign those with whom we disagree, especially if there is a history of disagreement.
- Realize that administrative leaders have a moral imperative to put student needs before staff preferences. Try to break out of your own pattern of thinking, especially before it becomes words you speak.

For administrators:

- Catch yourself before you pigeonhole individual teachers based on negative expectations you might have about them due to your history together. People can change—you can, the teacher can. As the leader, rebuilding trust must start with you.
- Use teachers' personal names, either with their titles (Mr. Smith, Dr. Jones), or better yet, their first names (Don, Donna) instead of just saying "Smith" or "Jones." This helps you connect as people rather than job titles.
- Do not stereotype teachers who are active union members. Think back to your own teaching days: Teachers may feel that you have forgotten what those days were like. Consider what common ground you can find between the teachers' concerns—whether they are citing the contract or not—and the goals of your initiative for students.
- Do not vilify teachers who disagree with you. Offer private forums for those who may appear to be intent on derailing your agenda in public; invite them to talk with you offline. Often a respectful, private conversation can unearth the personal agenda behind a behavior you find problematic.

Source: Wilhelm, T. (2013 February 26). *Teachers vs. Administrators: Ending the Adversarial Relationship*. Retrieved from http://education.cu-portland.edu/blog/leaders-link/teachers-vs-administrators-ending-the-adversarial-relationship/

A PROTOCOL FOR ■
UNCOMFORTABLE CONVERSATIONS

Kerry Patterson and his coauthors (2002) developed a simple protocol—STATE—for initiating and holding desperately needed but difficult conversations. Their book, *Crucial Conversations: Tools for Talking When Stakes Are High*, provides excellent background for using their model. STATE consists of three action steps and two reminders. In their book, the authors discuss the problem of stories—the stories we all tell ourselves about other people and their intentions. Relationships deteriorate as the stories become increasingly negative. As a leader initiates a difficult conversation, he or she has a desired outcome in mind—what the authors term a path to action. The individual who is engaged will also have a desired path, because that person also tells himself or herself stories about the leader.

Step 1 (Share your facts) is simple, as in "You've been late coming to our team meeting for three weeks." In Step 2 (Tell your story), the leader shares part of his or her "story" or interpretation of the facts, such as, "This makes me think you don't want to be part of our team or that you think our team's work is not important." In Step 3 (Ask for others' paths), the leader invites the other person to respond to what the leader just shared, inviting clarification and re-interpretation—as in "Am I right about that?" Steps 4 and 5 are reminders to "talk tentatively" and to "encourage testing." The leader should be prepared to hear perceptions about himself or herself that he or she may be unaware of. The authors stress that the purpose of a Crucial Conversation is the preservation and improvement of the relationship, not to impose a particular course of action or compliance with the leader's expectation. Timing is also important; these conversations are best held as soon as possible after the situation occurs, or as soon as a pattern begins to emerge. The agenda for this meeting will include a summary of STATE and a suggestion for practicing in the safe environment of the GC meeting.

Suggested Meeting Setup:

- Post the Questions of a PLC for reference
- Post the signed Norms poster

Agenda

Guiding Coalition Meeting

1. Review Norms and Assign Meeting Roles

2. Community Building

3. After Action Review

4. Working With Challenging Individuals

5. Tool Kit

6. Evaluate Norms

Note: There is no Team Planning agenda item since this meeting is devoted simply to responding to and working with challenging individuals.

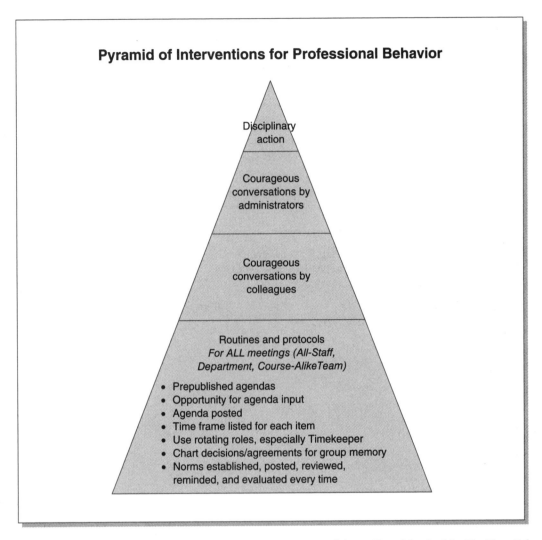

Pyramid of Interventions for Professional Behavior

Disciplinary action

Courageous conversations by administrators

Courageous conversations by colleagues

Routines and protocols
For ALL meetings (All-Staff, Department, Course-AlikeTeam)

- Prepublished agendas
- Opportunity for agenda input
- Agenda posted
- Time frame listed for each item
- Use rotating roles, especially Timekeeper
- Chart decisions/agreements for group memory
- Norms established, posted, reviewed, reminded, and evaluated every time

STATE Steps From
Crucial Conversations

- *Share your facts.* Start with the least controversial, most persuasive elements from your Path to Action.
- *Tell your story.* Explain what you're beginning to conclude.
- *Ask for others' paths.* Encourage others to share both their facts and their stories.
- *Talk tentatively.* State your story as a story, don't disguise it as a fact.
- *Encourage testing.* Make it safe for others to express differing or even opposing views.

Source: Patterson, K., Grenny, J., McMillan, R., & Switzler, A. (2002). *Crucial conversations: Tools for talking when stakes are high.* New York, NY: McGraw-Hill. Used with permission.

Eliminate E-mail for Problem Solving

- E-mail messages are easily misconstrued because the communicator is not present when the message is received; the receiver is free to "read into" the communication whatever he or she feels it represents.
- The majority of human communication is nonverbal; body language and voice tone communicate more than the words—all missing in an e-mail.
- Your e-mail message immediately becomes an artifact for the receiver to share and use as he or she pleases.
- E-mail messages virtually never solve problems; they create resentment and other undesirable responses in the receiver. Disharmony typically grows between the two parties.
- "E-mail wars" are begun when e-mail messages are forwarded to others who were not involved but are now interested in becoming involved.
- The natural time delay between e-mail being sent and received works against timely resolution of issues.
- Effective leaders do not solve problems using e-mail; they do the uncomfortable work person to person.
- E-mail should be used only to arrange a meeting, best without detailing the issue. Sometimes, an unexpected meeting is more effective.
- Instead of composing an e-mail, spend the time instead outlining your thoughts for yourself on paper, then practice beginning your conversation—use a mirror or role-play with a trusted partner. Anticipate possible responses and prepare for those as best you can, but realize that you can't anticipate everything. You **will** get better with practice.
- Taking the time to meet in person communicates that you care about the person, the relationship, and about making the situation better.
- If someone sends an e-mail to *you* attempting to engage you in a negative way, resist reacting and engaging. Reply instead, "Let's meet to talk about this. Are you available at _____?"

Suggested Materials and Equipment for Agenda

- Handouts, three-hole punched
  - Agenda
  - After Action Review
  - Pyramid of Interventions for Professional Behavior
  - STATE Steps from Crucial Conversations
  - Eliminate E-mail for Problem Solving
  - Professional Work Plan and Team Commitments for individual note taking, as desired

- Signed Norms poster
- Roles/Responsibilities tent cards
- After Action Review enlarged to poster size
- Chart rack, markers, tape
- Talking Stick
- Poster size copy of agenda posted (or projected)
- Questions of a PLC enlarged to poster size
- Professional Work Plan and Team Commitments enlarged to poster size, including additional copies of page 2 to include all teams
- Parking Lot enlarged to poster size and hung in the meeting area
- Sticky notes, 3x3 inches or larger for potential Parking Lot items
- Tool Kit poster with running list of tools introduced

■ AGENDA NOTES

Working With Challenging Individuals

As a way to introduce this topic, I ask the Recorder to draw a T-chart on the chart pad. The two columns will be called "Remarks" and "Our Team's Response." Then I invite team members to brainstorm remarks that are typical of resistors and other challenging individuals (e.g., "Whose idea was this?!"). Ask the Recorder to list these on the left side of the T-chart.

When the page is filled, the team to comes up with a leadership response to each remark (e.g., for the objection above, "The guiding coalition used the ideas we got from our teams!" or "Glad you asked! This is straight from the research on student engagement. Would you like to hear about it?"). Using humor that is not sarcastic will become a useful skill for team members to deflect naysayers' comments.

Once the team feels that the most common objections have been listed and dealt with, I take a few minutes to role-play. Although role-playing may feel weird at first to some team members, it is a very powerful way to practice new kinds of responses before being confronted by and using them with a strong, negative persona. I invite team members to pair up and take turns each being the resistor and the responding teacher leader, using the responses just brainstormed. If the team has an odd number of teacher leaders, I join the extra team member as partner.

Once the role-play is completed, I ask the team if they discovered other or better responses to the negative remarks, or if additional teacher objections/complaints and team responses have come to mind. The Recorder captures these additional ideas.

The Pyramid of Interventions for Professional Behavior handout is chiefly designed to focus a discussion on the critical importance of the pyramid's base—the everyday routines and procedures that GC members have begun to put in place in their team collaborations. These set expectations for professional behavior and also serve a preventive function against potential dysfunctional behavior.

Then, using the STATE handout, I invite each team member to take a moment to think of, and write down, a recent situation involving an issue with a teammate. Then, with either the same partner as before or a new one, role-play the three-step conversation.

Below is an excerpt from an article I coauthored with Dr. Maureen Latham, Superintendent of the Beaumont Unified School District, recounting an unrehearsed role-play we enacted for Beaumont's 10 K–adult school teams using this structure. Instructional Leadership Council (ILC) was the name of the group of teacher leaders and administrators who were leading the development of schools as professional learning communities through shared leadership. GLCs were grade-level chairs at the elementary level—already in place when ILC was formed, and some GLCs were not part of ILC.

Terry (as ILC team leader):	Maureen, we've been friends for a long time, and you've been the GLC for third grade for a long time, too. Lately, I'm feeling like we might be working at odds with each other in our team, and I think it's also affecting our friendship.
Maureen (as GLC):	I don't know what you're talking about.
Terry:	Well, last week, on our team meeting day, I asked everyone to bring their ideas for the new math assessment. Everyone was excited and brought great ideas, but you didn't bring anything.
Maureen:	I've told you and the others how busy I've been lately with everything going on at home.
Terry:	But that's not the first time you've come without anything to share. It was the same when we worked on our common assignments for science, and that wasn't the first time, either. It's starting to feel to me like you don't like me being a leader on the team, and maybe you want to be the only leader. Is that it?
Maureen:	Well, it does feel like you've been taking over.
Terry:	Maureen, I'm sorry if I've come across as taking over. What I really want is for us to lead our team together.
Maureen:	You've never asked me to work with you on leading our team.
Terry:	I'm asking you now.

At this point, we spontaneously hugged (not an unrealistic scenario for elementary teachers), and the room broke into relieved laughter, although it was only role-playing. We stressed that the outcome of such interchanges cannot necessarily be predicted; in opening a difficult conversation, it is entirely possible that we will receive information about *our own* behavior that needs to be changed.

From "Developing Principals to Create Shared Leadership," *Leadership,* January–February 2014, Association of California School Administrators. Reprinted with permission.

Finally, the Eliminate E-mail for Problem Solving handout highlights common problems that result from this medium. While e-mail might seem to be an attractive alternative to an uncomfortable conversation, it has so many drawbacks, including possible long-term negative ramifications between people; it should never be used for that purpose.

Tool Kit

The main purpose of this meeting is to give GC members new tools for working with challenging individuals. You may wish to invite them to add the following to their own and the team's Tool Kits: Team Responses for Our United Front, and Courageous Conversation (STATE) steps.

AFTER THE MEETING— ■
PRINCIPAL FOLLOW UP SUGGESTIONS

Daniel Heller's 2002 article, "The Power of Gentleness," serves as a wonderful reminder of the need for kindness and compassion on the part of school leaders. He recounts working individually with specific teachers, listening, and sometimes discovering personal issues that were impacting their professional performance. He describes one teacher as a "bitter complainer" and discovered that by simply listening—not by trying to provide solutions, for which she always had objections—the interactions gradually became more positive. Another teacher was going through a divorce. This is not to suggest that a leader pry into others' private lives, but through making an effort to learn something about each individual, healthy, positive *working* relationships develop. This is consistent with the research on school principals discussed in Chapter 8. One of the 21 Leadership Responsibilities identified in that research was termed *relationships*, with the definition "Demonstrates awareness of the personal aspects of teachers and staff." Teachers in the studies used in the meta-analysis identified this behavior as one of those that their effective principals exemplified.

TROUBLESHOOTING ■

What about those teachers who—regardless of your kind, compassionate, and courageous conversations, and those of the teacher leaders, and with all the practices in place in the pyramid's base—still refuse to budge? Many have said, "Kids can't wait." As you consider the Pyramid of Interventions for Professional Behavior, you may wonder about the pyramid's tip: disciplinary action. For good or ill, education stands in stark contrast to the business world, where refusal to adapt to company trends or comply with mandates and supervisor directives result in swift disciplinary action, including and up to termination. Historically, many districts have been reluctant to support principals in the documentation of unacceptable teacher behavior for all but the most egregious of offenses. Refusal to work as part of a team, behaving unprofessionally toward colleagues or in group meetings, or (most ironically) resisting changing classroom practices for the benefit of students are not usually considered severe enough to be documented. However, this is beginning to change in some districts.

Because of vast differences in district leadership, I strongly recommend that you work closely with your supervisor and the HR department if you decide to begin a documentation process. Obviously, this is the last step—the tip of the pyramid—after all other levels have been exhausted.

The good news is that even at the tip there are other steps available, which are not intended as disciplinary actions but ensure highly formalized, mandatory support, and send the unmistakable message that you are serious. Your district undoubtedly has some form of an assistance plan for teachers who are performing poorly. Once you have exhausted all other levels of the pyramid, do not hesitate to use that instrument since it is already in place in district and board policy. The biennial evaluation is another tool at your disposal. Ironically, many principals are often reluctant to mark any teacher as less than Good or even Exemplary in all the categories. Needs Improvement is rare, and Unsatisfactory is almost unheard of. Instead of following the expected tradition, use the appropriate categories of the evaluation tool to clearly communicate to the teacher that he or she is *not* performing acceptably, as well as to detail the support you are offering for this person to improve. If a Peer Assistance and Review (PAR) process is available, use it. Sometimes teachers respond very well to peers in a personal improvement process, especially if they are outside a teacher's own school. Finally, if all these fail, begin the documentation process once you are certain of district support. The students must come first. Your willingness to be persistent in holding frequent, uncomfortable conversations—and at some point, with the added ammunition of the tools mentioned—is the last bastion of hope for these teachers, and their students, to succeed. Will documentation result in termination? That is the intended endpoint of documentation systems, but in my observation and experience, once it is begun, most such teachers respond to the signal that the principal is serious and will usually decide to retire, resign, or move to another school where they can remain in their comfort zones. Sometimes even the less drastic measures such as assistance plans will have the same result.

Stresses on Your Teacher Leaders

Occasionally, a teacher leader will ask to be relieved of the duties of leading a collaborative team. A variety of factors may contribute to this decision, such as family demands, the additional layer of stress added by having to support peers in change efforts that already challenge the teacher leader personally, and/or the continuous tension of leading a team with one or more negative, resistant members. If this happens, it will feel disappointing, but you will need to quickly overcome your own feelings and do what you can to help the teacher feel that he or she is not a failure. Check in frequently with the teacher and reassure him or her that you continue to appreciate the contributions he or she is making.

Although you may not think that any other member of the team can lead it, it is important that the team continues to function as a collaborative team. Facilitator roles can rotate if necessary. Sit in with the team as often as you can to make sure this happens. Keep the team accountable by requiring the same products of them as you do for all the other teams. You do not need to immediately tap a new team leader, although you may find it is workable to do so. If you do, be prepared to spend your own time—and think of ways free up GC members, such as bringing in subs—to bring the new leader up to speed.

Coach Your Leaders

Never feel that you must have all the answers when a teacher leader brings you a problem. In fact, you may be depriving your leader of a chance to grow when you simply hand out a solution. Shared leadership is all about solving problems together. Paraphrase what you hear. Ask questions. Use multiples: "What are the kinds of ways you are thinking you might address that?" Offer suggestions if you have them, but let the teacher leader choose the solution that will work for the team that he or she knows far better than you do.

Collaboration Changes People

If you are able to persist in getting your resistant teachers to experience the benefits of collaboration, it will have amazing results for them and for their students. They will become not only amenable, but also eager to participate with their collaborative teams because it breaks down isolation, gives them built-in support groups, reduces the workload, *and* student learning will improve in their classes. High-level collaboration results in the emergence of new attitudes about students—yes, attitudes and beliefs can be changed as a result of new, positive experiences. Personal efficacy emerges and grows, replacing blaming of students and families. Some of the most highly effective teachers and team members I have met—some of whom now are administrators—were at one time resistors. Collaboration can transform schools, because it transforms people.

SUMMARY ■

This GC meeting agenda, which may be used anywhere in the sequence of meetings, provides a setting for the team to develop a united front for responding to negativity that may arise during complex change. It introduces the Pyramid of Interventions for Professional Behavior, with emphasis on the pyramid's base—the tools and routines that members now have at their disposal to help ensure professionalism during team meetings. Finally, using the STATE discussion structure gives GC members an opportunity to practice holding a difficult conversation with a colleague.

Access links and additional resources at
www.corwin.com/sharedleadership

17

Guiding
Coalition Meeting

Leading as Optimizers and Affirmers to Build Collective Efficacy

I saw an angel in the stone, and carved to set it free.

Michelangelo

A characteristic of schools that are advanced on the professional learning community (PLC) journey is teachers' widely held conviction that *all* students can achieve outcomes of significance. It is unusual for those working in traditional teacher isolation to hold this belief strongly, although exceptions occasionally emerge, such as Jaime Escalante, math teacher at Garfield High School, located in one of the most impoverished areas of Los Angeles, featured in the film *Stand and Deliver*.

Escalante's personal efficacy is evident throughout the film. Early on, he tells a class, "This is basic math, but basic math is too easy for you. So I'll teach you algebra, because I'm the champ." With both students and fellow staff, Escalante often referred to "ganas," which he defined as determination, discipline, and hard work. You may sometimes hear teachers complain they cannot teach the students who are not motivated. One of my favorite lines is that of Escalante saying to his students, "You don't have the ganas? I will give it to you, because I am an *expert*."

Unfortunately, even a Super Teacher working in isolation does not impact significant numbers of students. Escalante teamed with another teacher, Ben Jiménez, to begin the calculus program and eventually became chair of the math department, but lost the chairmanship and eventually left Garfield because of infighting and other staff issues, and student outcomes in math declined. Teamwork and *collective* efficacy and are key characteristics of schools that create and *sustain* the kind of momentum begun by Escalante.

How do you begin to cultivate teachers' belief in their own ability to reach and teach all students, and especially the belief that this is possible in their teams—this sense of personal and collective efficacy? Teachers' conscious and unconscious beliefs are powerful. The landmark Rosenthal Experiment in South San Francisco, resulting in the book *Pygmalion in the Classroom* by Rosenthal and Jacobson (1968), demonstrated the phenomenon of the self-fulfilling prophecy. The Teacher Expectations and Student Achievement (TESA) training program, developed at the Los Angeles County Office of Education, grew out of this study, based on the finding that teachers' subconscious behaviors toward students have a direct impact on their achievement.

As discussed in previous chapters, the most powerful way of changing beliefs is through new experiences. Albert Bandura (1977, 1986, 1995, 1997) pioneered work in building personal efficacy, and Roger Goddard and colleagues (2000, 2004, 2007, 2011, 2015) has done extensive research on teachers' collective efficacy. Both used the term *mastery experiences* for those experiences of success that help individuals gain belief in their personal or collective abilities.

Another method identified by Bandura and Goddard, social persuasion, also increases personal and collective efficacy. There are actions you can take right now in this area. First, assume the responsibility to begin collecting and publishing your own school's success stories, especially those of underperforming and special needs students. As educators, we tend to be so focused on the next mandate or initiative coming down the pike, we typically forget to celebrate the successes we do achieve. Publishing early successes—small, quick wins—is often key to keeping energy high in the all-important beginning stages of change, and certainly necessary for sustaining momentum. As discussed in Chapter 8, Marzano and fellow researchers (2005) termed this Responsibility Affirmation. Interestingly, as teachers described what principals did when leading effectively using Affirmation, some said their principal "systematically and fairly recognizes the failures of, and celebrates the accomplishments of the school as a whole" (pp. 41, 43–44). Not all the forays into new classroom practices will be immediately successful, but examining the failures and setbacks honestly, fairly, and without blaming is essential to progress.

Another Responsibility is termed Optimize. A principal who executes this Responsibility "inspires and leads new and challenging innovations," and "inspires teachers and staff to accomplish things that might be beyond their grasp" (Marzano, Waters, & McNulty, 2005, pp. 56–57). In shared leadership, teacher leaders as well as the principal must learn to lead as Optimizers.

Since your guiding coalition (GC) members each lead a team, they will share responsibility with you to collect student success stories. With each success, especially hard-won successes, teachers' sense of personal and collective efficacy will grow. Leaders accelerate this by continuing to remind people of what they have accomplished.

EXPLANATORY STYLE ■

Martin Seligman, author of *Learned Optimism: How to Change Your Mind and Your Life* (2006), coined the term "explanatory style." Individuals with a positive explanatory style tend to regard personal failures and setbacks as temporary, and specific to one, isolated situation ("OK, this didn't work, this time. Next time, I might . . ."). Individuals with a negative explanatory style tend to regard failures and setbacks as permanent and pervasive—that is, pervading every aspect of their lives ("This always happens to me. Nothing I do ever works."). Seligman discusses the critical importance of leaders' demonstrating a positive explanatory style to inspire those they lead with hope. As expressed by John William Gardner, "The first and last task of a leader is to keep hope alive."

I once worked with an elementary principal who was one of the most disabling administrators I have ever encountered due to her extremely negative explanatory style. In my first meeting with her, she launched almost immediately into a litany of reasons why her school was so tragically underperforming. They all involved the dysfunctions of poverty impacting the families of the students; none of them involved efforts, including tried-and-failed efforts, of herself or her staff to change school and classroom practices. I hoped that she was simply venting her discouragement to me as a consultant in this private setting, but as my work unfolded with this school, I observed that this was not the case. Her negative explanatory style enabled widespread excuse-making and was a major barrier to making even incremental changes in school-wide and classroom practices.

Being an Optimizer and using a positive explanatory style does not mean being phony, or failing to acknowledge the difficulties of the work. However, just as a coach whose team is predicted to be defeated cannot allow any defeatism to creep into her coaching, leaders are often called on to put on a game face and lead initiatives that at first blush may appear to be beyond the reach of those they lead. Reminding the team of the details of every past success that is in any way similar to the current challenge is one thing Optimizers do to rally their followers' energy and their belief that *this* success is entirely possible, however daunting. It is vital for the teacher leaders of your guiding coalition to be in concert with each other and with you in inspiring hope and belief in all the teachers on staff in their ability to accomplish great things with all students. Any teacher leader who may have a negative explanatory style needs your private, personal coaching. This GC meeting is devoted to the continued development of your teacher leaders as Optimizers and Affirmers. In addition to beginning immediately to collect and publish your school's hidden success stories, a second strategy is to examine and discuss true stories of those who have overcome significant odds in various areas of life and to consider what can be gained for your school's work from studying these examples.

■ PREPARING FOR THE GC MEETING: STORIES OF INSPIRATION

For this meeting, you will need a collection of true accounts of teams and individuals who have overcome significant odds. Sports is an obvious source, but your collection should span a wide range. There are examples in every realm of human endeavor, including education. One I use often is Reuven Feurstein, whose theory of Modifiable Intelligence led to his system of interventions for raising the cognitive development—growth measured by IQ scores—in brain damaged and cognitively handicapped individuals in Israel following World War II. Although his early results, showing improvements of 20–40 IQ points, were derided by fellow cognitive psychologists, as his body of work grew it came to be lauded and used worldwide. I encourage you to include his story in your collection for this agenda.

For a small team, you will need one story for each GC member. For larger GCs, such as secondary teams, make two to three copies of each story, and then each will be read by several members. Just Google Inspirational Stories or Overcoming Obstacles. Googling Beat the Odds will yield successful school stories, but be sure to collect stories outside education, too. The ideal length is about one blog-length page. The format of this meeting will be for you and the teacher leaders to create shared knowledge together.

Suggested Meeting Setup:

- Post the Questions of a PLC for reference
- Post the signed Norms poster

Agenda

Guiding Coalition Meeting

1. Review Norms and Assign Meeting Roles

2. Community Building

3. After Action Review

4. Leading as Optimizers and Affirmers

5. Team Planning

6. Tool Kit

7. Evaluate Norms

Leading as Optimizers and Affirmers

Optimize

Inspires others and is the driving force when implementing a challenging innovation

- Inspiring teachers to accomplish things that might be beyond their grasp
- Being the driving force behind major initiatives
- Portraying a positive attitude about the ability of staff to accomplish substantial things

Affirmation

Recognizes and celebrates school accomplishments and acknowledges failures

- Systematically and fairly recognizing the accomplishments of students
- Systematically and fairly recognizing the accomplishments of teachers
- Systematically and fairly recognizing the failures of the school as a whole

Explanatory Style*

Negative Explanatory Style: Permanent and Pervasive

- These students cannot learn.
- The families are too dysfunctional.
- They are not motivated, and I can't motivate the unmotivated.
- They are too far behind.
- Their IQs are too low.
- There is nothing I can do.
- It's my job to teach and their job to learn.
- I can't ruin their fragile self-esteem by giving them work that is too challenging.

Positive Explanatory Style: Temporary and Specific

- These students are capable—I/we have to find the right next step.
- My own teaching and the support of my team is stronger than the negative family and community influences.
- We can accelerate the learning of these students.
- IQ is not fixed and immutable.
- This unit was not successful for them, so my teammates and I will brainstorm new ways to engineer their learning.
- We are responsible for the learning of each of our students.
- Small, successful steps in rigorous, challenging work will help our students gain confidence as learners.

*Term coined by Martin Seligman (2006), *Learned Optimism: Changing Your Mind and Your Life.*

Paradigms/Mental Models

Definition:

Paradigms that have changed:

- The Earth is flat.
- The universe revolves around the Earth.
- People cannot rule themselves.
- Women do not have the capacity to vote with intelligence.
- Human beings cannot run a 4-minute mile.
- IQ is fixed and immutable.

Do we have any paradigms at our school that are barriers to our success with all students?

Stories of Inspiration—Note-Taking Guide

Was there a prevailing paradigm that this person or team had to overcome?

What other physical, mental, or emotional barriers had to be overcome?

What internal and external resources did the person or team call on to become successful?

What similarities are there in this story to our challenge of accomplishing outcomes of significance for *all* students?

What can we learn from this example for our own work?

What are the "Yeah, buts" that objectors might say to make this example irrelevant to our school? How might we respond?

Reflection

What are the implications of this information for me as a leader, as I lead my own team and interact with others on staff?

How might we use stories of inspiration to encourage our staff?

Suggested Materials and Equipment for Agenda

- Handouts, three-hole punched

  ○ Agenda
  ○ After Action Review
  ○ Leading as Optimizers and Affirmers, or refer to pp. 56–57 and 41–44 if you have purchased *School Leadership That Works* for GC members
  ○ Explanatory Style
  ○ Paradigms/Mental Models
  ○ Printouts of inspirational stories
  ○ Note-Taking Guide
  ○ Reflection page
  ○ Professional Work Plan and Team Commitments for individual note taking, as desired

- Signed Norms poster
- Roles/Responsibilities tent cards
- After Action Review enlarged to poster size
- Chart rack, markers, tape
- Talking Stick
- Poster size copy of agenda posted (or projected)
- Questions of a PLC enlarged to poster size
- Professional Work Plan and Team Commitments enlarged to poster size, including additional copies of page 2 to include all teams
- Parking Lot enlarged to poster size and hung in the meeting area
- Sticky notes, 3x3 inches or larger for potential Parking Lot items
- Tool Kit poster with running list of tools introduced

AGENDA NOTES ■

Leading as Optimizers and Affirmers

The handout defining these terms can be used to open a discussion of what examples (and non-examples) would look like in a school. I use the Explanatory Style handout to have team members brainstorm additional examples of both optimistic and pessimistic statements.

Team members can use their phones or other devices to do a search on the terms Paradigms and Mental Models. I ask the Recorder to chart some of the definitions that come up, then we wordsmith a team definition, and I invite members to record it on their handouts. Then we brainstorm additional examples of social and scientific paradigms/mental models that have changed. The real point of this handout is to discuss the question at the bottom: Do we have any paradigms at our school that are barriers to our success with all students?

At this point I distribute the various inspirational stories that I have collected for the team, and the Note-Taking Guide. I invite members to read the stories silently, making notes for sharing as they read. We share in round-robin fashion, with team members who read the same story contributing together. After everyone has shared, I ask the Recorder to chart common themes, using some or all the questions on the Note-Taking Guide.

Finally, I distribute the Reflection handout, inviting members to take a few minutes to silently write their own thoughts in response to the prompts. It is not necessary to have members share about the first prompt, but I extend the invitation in case anyone wishes to do so. Some members may see potential in using inspirational stories in a professional learning session with the staff. If so, the Recorder can chart these ideas from the second prompt and save them for the Professional Work Plan.

Tool Kit

The two tools you may invite GC members to add to their own and the team's Tool Kits are Positive Explanatory Style and Our School's Success Stories.

■ AFTER THE MEETING—PRINCIPAL FOLLOW UP SUGGESTIONS

Personal and collective efficacy are built when teachers achieve mastery experiences—hard-won successes with students. Thus, a leader must do everything possible to pave the way for those successes, through removing barriers and providing support such as material resources, professional learning, and coaching.

Increasingly effective teacher collaboration in your school will build collective efficacy. Goddard (2015) states,

> Teacher collaboration is a key to the pathway from leadership to collective efficacy beliefs because it is the shared interactions among group members that serve as the building blocks of collective efficacy. Strong instructional leadership can also serve to influence collective efficacy indirectly by setting normative expectations for formal, frequent, and productive teacher collaboration around instructional improvement. (p. 504)

Another high-leverage strategy for building personal and collective efficacy was termed *vicarious experience* by Bandura and Goddard. As a principal, I found this to be a most effective strategy for helping teachers who expressed that certain students were impossible. Sometimes this entailed having a coach go into a teacher's classroom and do demonstration lessons with the teacher's most difficult students. Visits to other classrooms can also be powerful, as long as someone accompanies the teacher to mediate the experience by pointing out specific behaviors of the teacher being observed, and/or share behind-the-scenes information about how the teacher planned and structured the learning and/or the classroom environment. Otherwise, the visiting teacher can easily say, "But I got all the tough kids." At the secondary level, having a teacher visit a colleague who has developed a positive relationship with a troublesome student, and observe the engagement and learning of this student in the other classroom, can help the visiting teacher understand what may be leading to the problems with the student in his or her classroom. As trust is built within teacher teams, visits to each other's classrooms can become a spontaneous and frequent occurrence.

Having systematic interventions in place (Chapter 15) at the classroom, team, and school-wide level is a vital aspect of building collective efficacy. That development, as well as employing strategies mentioned in this chapter, will greatly boost teachers' belief in their collective ability to attain outcomes of significance for every student.

SUMMARY ■

Having a positive explanatory style and behaving as Optimizers and Affirmers are critical for school leaders, but they do not come naturally to everyone. This GC meeting will focus on understanding these terms. In addition, your facilitation of a discussion of true, inspirational stories is designed to create a renewed sense of what is possible. Your team may decide to replicate this activity with the entire staff.

Access links and additional resources at
www.corwin.com/sharedleadership

18

Sustaining a Culture of Shared Leadership

You have now established a culture of shared leadership in your school, and ownership of professional learning community (PLC) processes continues to grow among all staff members. Teachers have de-privatized their practice and are no longer isolated behind their classroom doors. They regard all the students within their teams—and increasingly, school-wide—as *our students*. Systematic, systemic interventions target students' immediate learning gaps and address both academic and emotional/behavioral needs. The cumulative result is that it is now all but impossible for any student to fall through the cracks, achievement gaps have closed or are rapidly closing, and all student outcomes show ongoing improvement. Students who have always been high performing are not allowed to rest on their laurels because teachers challenge them with ever-more-rigorous, engaging opportunities to extend and enrich their learning.

Similar to an individual lifestyle change—moving, for example, to a healthier diet and regular exercise—the culture you have created with your teacher leaders will not sustain itself automatically. Slipping back into old patterns is alarmingly easy because the historical roots of traditional practices in education are deep and strong.

■ CONTINUED DEVELOPMENT OF SHARED LEADERSHIP

By now, guiding coalition (GC) members, who already each lead teams of their own, have ample preparation to co-facilitate GC meetings with you and with each other—perhaps they have already begun to do so. *But this does not mean that you can now withdraw from involvement!* In developing shared leadership, you move gradually from center stage facilitation to participating fully as a team member. I recall working with two different teams, each with leaders who habitually left the room to take phone calls or attend to other matters during team meetings, appointing someone in the group to take charge in the meantime. These were high-functioning teams with formal meeting norms in place, but interestingly, this leader behavior served as a signal for people to disengage. Others would leave the room, too, and almost everyone became focused on their cell phones or other devices while the current agenda item ostensibly continued under the appointed facilitator. In hindsight, I think that symbolically, in exiting the meeting, each leader unwittingly conveyed a personal hierarchy of importance. Phone call (or whatever): important; this team and team meeting: not that important. These leaders did share leadership to a limited extent, but this set of behaviors was not about sharing leadership. It was about personal preference and convenience.

Am I saying that the GC should never meet without you? Remember that you are *sharing* leadership, not abdicating leadership. That said, at this stage, I believe that if an extremely urgent reason compelled you to be unavailable during a scheduled GC meeting, you could very strategically arrange for it to go ahead as planned. First, if there are not already one or more teacher leaders scheduled to facilitate, survey the group for volunteers. Do not appoint a facilitator. Why? Almost everyone else will wonder why you did not tap them for the role. Second, review the agenda to make sure there is no item on which discussion or progress will be impaired or halted by your absence. Third, arrange a debrief meeting with two to three members—logically, including the facilitator(s)—to take place as soon as feasibly possible afterward. Even when you have empowered the GC to make specific decisions without you, using clearly set parameters, it is essential that its members know that you always remain fully in the communication loop. As you make these arrangements, explicitly communicate your high level of trust to the team, as well as your commitment to the ongoing development of shared leadership. Finally, let this be a rare occurrence only.

Given the superhuman level of expectations and responsibilities placed on today's principals, no principal can function effectively without knowing how to delegate tasks and responsibilities. But shared leadership is not the same as delegation. Shared leadership is developed thoughtfully and strategically over time, with an ongoing relationship of coleading as budding leaders grow in experience and expertise, and with gradual release of control by the principal as it is assumed by new leaders. In contrast, delegation is simply passing off a task or responsibility to someone who is willing and able to complete or fulfill it. Working with your guiding coalition is not a commitment you can now delegate to someone else, such as an assistant principal. Nor can you simply slip away after GC members begin rotating responsibility for facilitating the meetings. It is essential to keep sacred time carved out for working with your teacher leaders, even if it is less frequent than in the beginning, because *everything* you have put in place together in your school requires maintenance, ongoing evaluation, and sometimes modification. Best practice meeting routines, regular cycles of teams coming to agreement on essential learnings and developing common assessments, setting SMARTe goals and analyzing results are all *nontraditional* school activities that require continued energy and attention to be sustained. The tiers of your Pyramid Response to Intervention require continuous monitoring and refinement. Think of the investment you, your teacher leaders, and your staff have made to put all this in place. None of it will be sustained on autopilot. Since you already have a vehicle for monitoring the work of teams through regular After Action Reviews at the beginning of each GC meeting, it only makes sense to continue to use that effective tool to help ensure maintenance of what is in place.

Your teacher leaders still need your personal support and continued development in their own leadership. Although you can now delegate more tasks and responsibilities to GC members as you judge that they are ready—and, of course, willing—new aspects of shared leadership will emerge that will continue to require gradual development. For example, after a period of cochairing an ad hoc committee with a GC member, you may eventually delegate that role to the teacher leader to fulfill solo. However, the same teacher leader may be very reluctant to address the full staff, or to facilitate any sort of full-staff professional learning activity, but may wish to become confident and competent in doing so. You develop that leader's capacity by co-planning small steps, being present and visible for moral support while he or she is in front of the group, and debriefing afterward.

As stated, you cannot delegate the responsibility to continue to meet with your GC members as a team and to work with them as needed individually. Your involvement will always be important to the rest of the staff as well. Without your ongoing communication about expectations you are tight on, it is easy for staff members to begin to assume, "Oh, I guess we're not doing that anymore." This is how best practice meeting routines and team planning cycles are gradually abandoned, how progress monitoring of students in interventions deteriorates, and how interventions themselves fade and disappear.

In a shared leadership school, your guiding coalition will continue to fulfill the important roles of serving as your chief advisory group and being a critical body for ensuring strong, two-way communication with the staff. As you and your leaders approach new initiatives—for example, an examination of your school's grading practices in light of current research—GC members are the natural choice to be the ones to spearhead the investigation and the building of shared knowledge with the rest of the staff. Professional readings can be an important part of building shared knowledge. For professional reading protocols with groups see the Resource Articles and Videos section of the companion website.

■ A LEADER-FUL SCHOOL

In a shared leadership school, keep your sights on the goal of having every teacher—and every staff member—become a leader. This may feel like a stretch goal if you still have a few resistors, but in my experience it is an entirely sound goal. Not everyone must become a member of the guiding coalition to be a leader. Consider this: What are other areas where you have not yet begun to share leadership? At Kinard Middle School in Fort Collins, Colorado, a new teacher said, "Right away, I was told, 'Just because you're new doesn't mean you aren't a leader.'" At KMS, the message is clear: Everyone has expertise. You are expected to be a leader and to develop both your areas of expertise and your leadership. Finally, how can you develop the leadership of your office staff, your custodial staff, and other nonteaching personnel?

As the work evolves at your school, you may find that you need to augment the membership of the guiding coalition, or replace members who move away, retire, or simply ask to take a hiatus from the responsibilities of GC membership and team leadership. Remember also that collaborative teacher teams can be co-led by a new and outgoing team leader, providing a natural transition. How will you select new GC members?

In the Beaumont Unified School District, the district and site leaders came to agreement that with the transition to Common Core State Standards, it was time to augment the Instructional Leadership Council or ILC (see discussion on naming your guiding coalition in Chapter 1). I developed this job description with principals' input to help them select and recruit new ILC members.

Instructional Leadership Council

Member Job Description

Member Purpose:

To function as an active team member to move the school ahead
toward continuously improving outcomes for every student
and become a highly skilled teacher leader and model for peers.

Member Responsibilities

- Attend ILC meetings with the team, and participate fully in all activities.
- Suspend judgments, presume positive intentions, and keep an open mind for new ideas that may not fit past paradigms.
- Balance advocating for specific actions with asking questions to clarify others' points of view.
- Listen to facilitators and team members with a genuine willingness to learn and grow.
- When intersession meetings are held back at the site, attend with the team to debrief new material and plan for next steps with school teams and the full staff.
- Be willing to lead or colead collaborative teams using new skills learned at ILC meetings.
- Be willing to facilitate activities with the full staff along with fellow ILC members and administrators and be willing to try out and model new instructional strategies for colleagues.
- Be prepared to present a united front with the team and administrators in modeling and advocating for new actions agreed on by the team.
- Speak in positive ways about new initiatives, even while acknowledging difficulties. Continue to encourage others, even in the face of resistance or negativity.
- Act in courageous ways for the benefit of students.
- Serve for 2 years, based on fulfillment of this job description. This is a voluntary position.

You may be wondering why I didn't share this with you back in Chapter 1 when I discussed The Right Team. It is simply because when shared leadership and PLC processes are new and relatively unheard of, using a job description such as this will probably garner very few takers. I offer it now, not as something to publish, but to help you with discussion points as you meet with new, potential GC members.

■ ASSIMILATING NEW STAFF MEMBERS

Because of our deeply rooted traditions in education, one thing that can unexpectedly weaken your culture is the introduction of new staff members. Over time, you will gain new teachers—some newly minted, recent college graduates, others who are new hires but have experience, and still others who transfer to your school from other schools in the district. Transfers may be voluntary or involuntary. Let's look at one group at a time to understand where problems may arise.

New Teachers

Teachers new to the profession are typically open, even eager to try just about anything their colleagues and administrators suggest. A culture of strong team collaboration is a distinct advantage for teachers who are brand new to the profession. Instead of struggling through their first year alone, hiding their inadequacies and being afraid to ask for help or even ask questions, these lucky teachers have a built-in support system. The teachers in your school who have created highly effective teams will be welcoming and happy to mentor their new colleagues.

However, new teachers can be especially vulnerable to the friendly advances of any remaining naysayers, who have by now lost their power base and would welcome the opportunity to take a neophyte under their wing and have someone to influence once again. A third-year elementary principal lamented to me, "This year I finally got to hire some new teachers because we had some retirements last year. I see them being poisoned before my very eyes." Unfortunately, she had not begun to share leadership and her school was not on the PLC journey so collaboration was not in place. But be aware that negative influences can quickly impact your impressionable new teachers, even in a school with positive, collaborative culture.

Experienced New Staff Members—New Hires

In my experience, experienced new hires, like beginning teachers, are typically open to suggestions and feedback from the administrator who hires them, at least for a while. This creates a natural opportunity for you to begin to acclimate them to your school's culture, beginning with the hiring process. If your district HR department allows you to personalize the standard set of district interview questions for your school, you can add questions about the candidate's experience with common assessments, sharing of data and classroom practices, and team collaboration in general.

In spite of this, it is possible to be surprised. A candidate who fielded these questions well and seemed open to working in a culture like your school's, and whose references were entirely positive, may turn out to be quite different than you were led to believe, once they move into a classroom on your campus. Unlike beginning teachers, these new hires have already formed habits and beliefs based on their experience at other schools, and being hired for your school may present second order change for them on multiple fronts.

Experienced New Staff Members—Transfers

Voluntary transfers normally signal some attraction that drew an experienced teacher from another district site to your school. It could be that he or she has heard about your new, strong, positive culture, or it could be that your school is closer to the day care location for the teacher's own children, closer to home, or otherwise more desirable than his or her previous school for a variety of personal reasons. Don't assume that an experienced teacher who voluntarily transfers to your site will easily step into a collaborative role in a team setting. Like experienced new hires, they may have habits and beliefs that mitigate against a smooth transition to your school.

Involuntary transfers may hold the greatest potential for causing disequilibrium in your school's culture. Involuntary transfers occur for a variety of reasons, including loss of funding and loss of enrollment, and the contract will dictate how they are carried out.

The tradition of placing teachers by seniority rather than by site or student needs is still deeply entrenched in the contract language of many districts. When funding or enrollment is declining, newer teachers who have become enthusiastic members of collaborative teams may be displaced by more senior teachers from traditional sites that are not PLCs and where leadership is not shared. This can cause significant disruption to team processes. Worse, some of these teachers may have no wish to be transferred to your site, but must accept the transfer to remain employed.

A Potential New Audience for Complaining

It almost goes without saying that negaholics always seem to find each other. By now, those who were resistors on your staff have become, for the most part, functional team members and have lost their edge of public negativity because of consistent messages from both peers and administrators that it is not acceptable. But new faces on the staff present a new opportunity for negativity that has gone underground to reemerge, and if a newcomer—perhaps an involuntary transfer—seems to be a kindred spirit, the attraction will be practically irresistible.

Actions That Can Help

Even with no potential for negativity presented by adding new staff members to the mix, the mere addition of new players who are unused to your teams' routines and protocols, and the specific behaviors expected in your culture can serve to weaken them. What can you do to ensure that this does not happen?

The Importance of Regular Maintenance

Teachers understand the importance of investing time at the beginning of the school year to teaching routines and procedures to students in their classes, even if some of the students may have been in classes with them before. In this regard, adults in organizations have similar needs—a regular review, at least annually, of routines and procedures is important to remind everyone of these expectations, and to acclimate new staff members in "how we do things here." Mini-reviews are helpful at the semester break at the secondary level, when team membership may be shifting due to changes in class assignments, as well as the possibility of a small number of new hires due to changed needs in the master schedule. Once on a visit to a high school tenth-grade English team during collaboration, I noticed that the team Norms poster sported a new addition—more obvious because it had been written in a different color marker than the original set. It said, "No complaining without a suggestion." I knew that an infamously negative teacher had had his class schedule changed at the semester and had joined this very effective team. While I generally advocate wording norms in positive language, I understood the bluntness of the added norm, considering the need the team had to help this particular individual adjust his behavior appropriately to their collaborations.

Before school ends in May or June, be sure to calendar an agenda item during a GC meeting to plan for back-to-school review in August or September of "how we do things here." This will serve as a reminder for continuing staff members that these expectations are still in place and to inform new staff members about key behaviors that are valued in your school's culture. Some of this review can be conducted whole-staff with GC members co-facilitating, and some can be done during individual team collaborations when teams actually engage in the work of reevaluating their norms, agreeing on essential learnings, and developing common assessments for the first units of study.

Buddy Teachers Help Acclimate New Staff Members

In addition to reminding teams to provide extra support to new members, a wise course of action is to pair up new hires with Buddy Teachers. Although the new teachers may have formal mentors assigned—for example, to support them through completion of a state induction program—those mentors typically have a task-specific relationship with their assigned new teachers and may be from other schools around the district.

A Buddy Teacher is simply an informal, go-to friend on campus. In the case of a new teacher, this colleague helps the new teacher with school procedures and can answer the plethora of questions that arise in the first year of teaching. Members of the collaborative team will offer many kinds of informal support as well, but having a designated Buddy Teacher can help the new teacher feel less awkward about asking questions and expressing needs. As you select and personally invite individual teachers to be Buddy

Teachers, you will seek out those who are positive about your school's new culture and can help acclimate the new teacher to its expectations. This will help offset potential influences of less positive individuals who may also decide to befriend him or her.

A Buddy Teacher is also a viable option for new staff members who are experienced, but the Buddy Teacher's role can be of a shorter duration. Watch for signals that the newly transferred teacher, or experienced new hire, is experiencing difficulty adjusting to your culture, and be prepared to spend time personally with the teacher in your balanced leadership stance as described in previous chapters.

As you broaden the opportunities for teacher leadership in your school, remember to consider teachers who may not be on the guiding coalition, but who would be strong models and positive Buddy Teachers for new staff members.

Supporting Collaborative Teams With New Members

Pay particular attention to the teams that have new members—new hires or transfers, voluntary or involuntary. In addition to allocating extra time to sitting in and observing/coaching the team during collaborations, stay in close touch with their team leaders to provide additional individual leadership coaching as needed.

CONTINUE YOUR OWN DEVELOPMENT AS A LEADER

How can you be sure that you continue to be a leader with whom others wish to share leadership? Debbie Fay, mentioned in Chapter 16, developed a simple method for use at the end of each school year to help ascertain the impact of her leadership on her staff. At the end of the last, or next-to-last staff meeting, she would tell her teachers that she needed their feedback so that she could continue to grow as a leader. She asked them to respond to two questions regarding her planning for the coming fall: What are you afraid I'll do? What are you afraid I won't do? There were no ratings, and the two-item survey was anonymous, although as trust developed, many of the teachers signed their surveys anyway. Debbie left an envelope on a table, asking that all surveys be completed and put into the envelope before leaving the meeting. She didn't look at them until a couple of weeks later, after the teachers had left for the summer and she was ready to think about her fall planning. She says, "It was interesting. Sometimes, on different surveys, the same answer would appear for both questions, such as 'change my team.'" Some answers dealt with student issues, such as tardies, but most had to do with her leadership of adults, such as "Don't become top-down" or "I hope you never start disciplining people instead of coaching them." It takes considerable courage for a leader to open herself or himself up to possible criticism, especially providing an opportunity to give it anonymously, but an action like Debbie's conveys a principal's great respect for the teachers he or she leads.

■ YOUR LEGACY AS A SHARED LEADERSHIP PRINCIPAL

As you create a leader-ful school, you are greatly enhancing the durability of the systems you develop together. The more leaders you have, the more sustainable the systems. Some of your teacher leaders will move into administration, and you will lose them. This is both part of the legacy you are creating for the benefit of students and staff in other schools, and part of the process of growing an ever-stronger network of newer leaders who will move into their shoes in your school. Of all the positions I held as a full-time member of the public education system in California for 36 years, the principalship was the most intensely rewarding. It was also incredibly demanding, very difficult at times, and sometimes very lonely. Remember that not all leadership can be shared, just as not all information you are privy to can be shared. But shared leadership is not for the purpose of reducing your own burden, although eventually it may have exactly that effect. As one principal said, "It's not just my voice anymore." But the ultimate purpose of shared leadership is to enhance and improve the overall leadership of your school for the benefit of the students you serve. Your school will be vastly better under authentically shared leadership than under your leadership alone. Your teachers can and should be your partners so that your school continuously becomes the very best it can be for students. The demands on schools are greater than they have ever been, but when leadership is shared, schools can rise to the challenges, because together we can accomplish what none of us can accomplish alone.

■ SUMMARY

Now that your school operates as a fully functional PLC under shared leadership, it must be maintained and sustained to prevent regression into old habits and practices. As new faces appear on staff, it is critical to acclimate them to the expectations and behaviors of being members of a professional learning community. Whole-staff reviews and reminders are also important to maintain a common language and to keep these expectations at the forefront of a dynamic milieu of new educational mandates and initiatives. Finally, your own development as a shared leadership principal must continue for you to remain effective as the Learning Leader of your school.

 Access links and additional resources at
www.corwin.com/sharedleadership

References and Resources

Bandura, A. (1977). Self-efficacy: Toward a unifying theory of behavioral change. *Psychological Review, 84*(2), 191–215.

Bandura, A. (1986). *Social foundations of thought and action*. Englewood Cliffs, NJ: Prentice Hall.

Bandura, A. (1995). *Self-efficacy in changing schools*. Cambridge, England: Cambridge University Press.

Bandura, A. (1997). *Self-efficacy: The exercise of control*. New York, NY: W. H. Freeman.

Barth, R. (2001). *Learning by heart*. San Francisco, CA: Jossey-Bass.

Barth, R. (2002). The culture builder. *Educational Leadership, 59*(8), 6–11.

Barth, R. (2003). *Lessons learned: Shaping relationships and the culture of the workplace*. Thousand Oaks, CA: Corwin.

Barth, R. (2006). Improving relationships within the schoolhouse. *Educational Leadership, 63*(6), 8–13.

Barth, R. (2013). The time is ripe (again). *Educational Leadership, 71*(2), 10–14, 16.

Bass, B. M., & Bass, R. (2008). *The Bass handbook of leadership: Theory, research, and managerial applications*. New York, NY: Free Press.

Buffum, A., & Mattos, M. (Eds.). (2014). *It's about time: Planning interventions and extensions in elementary school*. Bloomington, IN: Solution Tree.

Buffum, A., Mattos, M., & Weber, C. (2009). *Pyramid response to intervention: RtI, Professional learning communities, and how to respond when kids don't learn*. Bloomington, IN: Solution Tree.

Buffum, A., Mattos, M., Weber, C., & Hierck, T. (2014). *Uniting academic and behavior interventions: Solving the skill or will dilemma*. Bloomington, IN: Solution Tree.

California Department of Education. (2013). *Essential program components*. Retrieved from http://www.cde.ca.gov/ta/ac/ti/essentialcomp.asp

Carroll, T., Fulton, K., & Doerr, H. (2010). *Team up for 21st century teaching & learning: What research and practice reveal about professional learning*. Washington, DC: National Commission on Teaching and America's Future.

Covey, S. (2004, 1989). *The 7 habits of highly effective people: Powerful lessons in personal change*. New York, NY: Free Press.

DuFour, R. (2007). We're already a "good" school; why do we need to improve? Retrieved from http://www.allthingsplc.info/blog/view/16/wersquore-already-a-good-school-why-do-we-need-to-improve

DuFour, R. (2015). *In praise of American educators and how they can become even better*. Bloomington, IN: Solution Tree.

DuFour, R., & DuFour, R. (2012). *Professional learning communities at work: Bringing the big ideas to life*. Conference booklet. Indian Wells, CA.

DuFour, R., DuFour, R., Eaker, R., & Many, T. (2010). *Learning by doing: A handbook for professional learning communities at work* (2nd ed.). Bloomington, IN: Solution Tree.

DuFour, R., & Fullan, F. (2013). *Cultures built to last: Systemic PLCs at work.* Bloomington, IN: Solution Tree.

DuFour, R., & Marzano, R. (2011). *Leaders of learning: How district, school, and classroom leaders improve student achievement.* Bloomington, IN: Solution Tree.

DuFour, R., & Sparks, D. (1991). *The principal as staff developer.* Bloomington, IN: Solution Tree.

Fullan, M. (2013). *Stratosphere: Integrating technology, pedagogy, and change knowledge.* Toronto, Ontario: Pearson Canada.

Goddard, R., Goddard, Y., Sook Kim, E., & Miller, R. (2015). A theoretical and empirical analysis of the roles of instructional leadership, teacher collaboration, and collective efficacy beliefs in support of student learning. *American Journal of Education, 121*(4), 501–530.

Goddard, Y., Goddard, R., & Tschannen-Moran, M. (2007). A theoretical and empirical investigation of teacher collaboration for school improvement and student achievement in public elementary schools. *Teachers College Record, 109*(4), 877–896.

Goddard, R., Hoy, W., & Hoy, A. (2000). Collective teacher efficacy: Its meaning, measure, and impact on student achievement. *American Educational Research Journal, 37*(2), 479–507.

Goddard, R., LoGerfo, L., & Hoy, W. (2004). High school accountability: The role of perceived collective efficacy. *Educational Policy, 18*(3), 403–425.

Goddard, R., & Salloum, S. J. (2011). Collective efficacy beliefs, organizational excellence, and leadership. In G. M. Spreitzer & K. S. Cameron (Eds.), *The Oxford handbook of positive organizational scholarship* (pp. 642–650). Oxford, UK: Oxford University Press. doi: 10.1093/oxfordhb/9780199734610.013.0048

Hallinger, P. (2003). Leading educational change: reflections on the practice of instructional and transformational leadership. *Cambridge Journal of Education, 33,* 329–352.

Hattie, J. (2009). *Visible learning: A synthesis of over 800 meta-analyses relating to achievement.* New York, NY: Routledge.

Hattie, J. (2015). *What doesn't work in education: The politics of distraction.* London, UK: Pearson.

Heller, D. (2002). The power of gentleness. *Educational Leadership, 59*(8), 76–79.

Hord, S., Lloyd, J., Roussin, L., & Sommers, W. (2010). *Guiding professional learning communities: Inspiration, challenge, surprise, and meaning.* Thousand Oaks, CA: Corwin.

Institute of Education Sciences. (n.d.). What works clearinghouse. http://ies.ed.gov/ncee/wwc/

Lambert, L. (2002). Beyond instructional leadership: A framework for shared leadership. *Educational Leadership, 59,* 37–40.

Latham, M., & Wilhelm, T. (2014). Supporting principals to create shared leadership. *Leadership, 43*(3), 22–26, 38.

Lewis, C., & Hurd, J. (2011). *Lesson study step by step: How teacher learning communities improve instruction.* Portsmouth, NH: Heinemann.

Lindahl, R. (2008). Shared leadership: Can it work in schools? *Educational Forum, 72,* 298–307.

Locust, C. (n.d.). The talking stick. Retrieved from https://www.acaciart.com/stories/archive6.html

Los Angeles County Office of Education—TESA training. (n.d.). Retrieved from http://www.lacoe.edu/Home/CommunityServices/ParentCommunityServices/TESA.aspx

Marks, H., & Printy, S. (2003). Principal leadership and school performance: An integration of transformational and instructional leadership. *Educational Administration Quarterly, 39,* 370–397.

Marzano, R. (2003). *What works in schools: Translating research into action.* Alexandria, VA: ASCD.

Marzano, R. (2006). *Classroom assessment & grading that work.* Alexandria, VA: ASCD.

Marzano, R., Waters, T., & McNulty, B. (2005). *School leadership that works: From research to results.* Alexandria, VA: ASCD.

Patterson, K., Grenny, J., McMillan, R., & Switzler, A. (2002). *Crucial conversations: Tools for talking when stakes are high.* New York, NY: McGraw-Hill.

Platt, A. D., Tripp, C. E., Fraser, R. G., Warnock, J. R., & Curtis, R. E. (2008). *Transforming ineffective teams: Maximizing collaboration's impact on learning (The skillful leader II).* Acton, MA: Ready About Press.

Printy, S., & Marks, H. (2006). Shared leadership for teacher and student learning. *Theory Into Practice, 45,* 125–132.

Reeves, D. (2011). Webinar: Closing the implementation gap. Retrieved from http://www.leadandlearn.com/sites/default/files/presentation_slides/110124-056-closing-implementation-gap_1.pdf

Richardson, J. (2011). The ultimate practitioner. *Phi Delta Kappan, 93*(1), 27–32.

Rosenthal, R., & Jacobson, L. (1968). *Pygmalion in the classroom: Teacher expectation and pupils' intellectual development.* Carmarthen, Wales, UK: Crown House.

Schmoker, M. (1999a). *Results: The key to continuous school improvement* (2nd ed.). Alexandria, VA: ASCD.

Schmoker, M. (1999b). *Results: The key to continuous school improvement.* Workshop booklet. Riverside, CA.

Seligman, M. E. P. (2006). *Learned optimism: How to change your mind and your life.* New York, NY: Random House.

U.S. Department of Education, Office of Special Education, Technical Assistance Center on Positive Behavioral Interventions and Supports. (n.d.). Retrieved from www.pbis.org

Wahlstrom, K. L., & Louis, K.S. (2008). How teachers experience principal leadership: the roles of professional community, trust, efficacy, and shared responsibility. *Educational Administration Quarterly, 44,* 458–495.

Waters, T., & Cameron, G. (2007). *The balanced leadership framework: Connecting vision with action.* Denver, CO: Mid-Continent Research for Education and Learning.

Waters, T., Cameron, G., Lyons, C., & Eck, J. (2009). *Balanced leadership—Managing change* (Participants' manual). Denver, CO: Mid-Continent Research for Education and Learning.

Waters, T., Cameron, G., McIver, M., & Eck, J. (2009a). *Balanced leadership—An overview* (Facilitators' manual). Denver, CO: Mid-Continent Research for Education and Learning.

Waters, T., Cameron, G., McIver, M., & Eck, J. (2009b). *Balanced leadership—An overview* (Participants' manual). Denver, CO: Mid-Continent Research for Education and Learning.

Wilhelm, T. (2010). Fostering shared leadership. *Leadership, 40*(2), 22–24, 34, 36, 38.

Wilhelm, T. (2013). How principals cultivate shared leadership. *Educational Leadership, 71*(2), 62–66.

Wilhelm, T. (n.d.). *Leaders' Link* online column for principals, assistant principals, and district level leaders. Archived at http://education.cu-portland.edu/category/blog/leaders-link/

Index

CORWIN
A SAGE Publishing Company

CORWIN HAS ONE MISSION: to enhance education through intentional professional learning.

We build long-term relationships with our authors, educators, clients, and associations who partner with us to develop and continuously improve the best evidence-based practices that establish and support lifelong learning.

Solutions you want. Experts you trust. Results you need.